I0408960

THE DIVORCE FIREWALL STRATEGY

*How to Avoid Losing Everything
In a Divorce By Planning Ahead*

Jeffrey G. Marsocci, Esq.

Domestic Partner Publishing, LLC

For more information, go to www.DivorceFirewall.com

Note regarding legal counsel

As with any product, it is important to be clear about its intended purpose and use to avoid any misunderstandings. Specifically with writings about legal issues, it is noted that these materials are not a substitute for competent legal counsel. The contents of this guide are instead written to provide information about common estate planning problems, and it is designed for general educational purposes only. The contents of this guide are not to be construed as legal advice, and no attorney-client privilege exists between the reader and the author and/or publisher. In addition, laws change frequently, and therefore you also are urged to speak with an attorney about changes in the law that may affect you.

Circular 230 Disclosure: To ensure compliance with requirements imposed by the Internal Revenue Service, unless specifically indicated otherwise, any tax advice contained in this communication (including any accompanying literature) was not intended or written to be used, and cannot be used, for the purpose of avoiding tax-related penalties or promoting, marketing, or recommending to another party any tax-related matter addressed herein. For specific legal advice, you are urged to contact an attorney in your state or jurisdiction.

About the Author

Jeffrey G. Marsocci was born in Fort Worth, Texas, and raised in Lincoln, Rhode Island, where he graduated from Mount Saint Charles Academy High School. He received his Bachelor's degree in Business from Hofstra University, and two years later earned his law degree from the same university.

In 2004, he received a Certificate Degree in Non-Profit Management from Duke University, and has earned his Legal Master of Estate Preservation designation from the *Abts Institute for Estate Preservation*. Jeff also served as a member of the Legal Council for The Estate Planning Source, LLC, a nationally recognized estate preservation company formed by the protégés of the late Henry W. Abts III, trust guru and author of *The Living Trust*.

Mr. Marsocci has led his own firm in Raleigh, North Carolina, since 1996, focusing on the areas of Trusts and Estate Planning with a concentration on helping his clients plan ahead to avoid problems rather than clean them up afterwards. He also frequently participates in national and regional programs to educate attorneys, financial advisors and accountants on estate planning issues.

Jeff and his wife Kathleen are active volunteers in the community, and they frequently work with civic groups and other non-profits. Jeff and Kathy also each received the President's Call to Service Award for performing more than 4,000 hours of service during their lifetimes.

This book is dedicated to those friends and family who lost more than they should have in a divorce, and those who suffer in silence because it's "cheaper to keep her."

TABLE OF CONTENTS

For more information, go to www.DivorceFirewall.com

Introduction

The stories emerge every day. A couple meets, dates, and he falls hard for her. He does all the romantic things he was always told to by bringing her flowers, taking her on expensive dates, and they move in together. Eventually in 2008, he gets down on one knee in front of their family and friends, surrounded by rose petals at sunset on the beach, and he proposes in an Instagram-worthy fashion if Instagram would have been a thing back then.

This is the fictional story of Bill Peterson. Fifteen years later it is 2023, and Bill is now a 45-year-old financial advisor who lost big in a divorce with his wife Karen. Bill was raised by his single mom with a largely absent father, and he was always taught to revere women, put them on a pedestal, and to become the Prince Charming that will one day find his princess. That princess was Karen. She was "The One" that his mother, grandmother, aunts and other women in his life always told him to be on the lookout for. But how did Bill get here?

When he was growing up, Bill went about doing everything that the women in his life told him to do. He went to college, majored in economics, but then went to get a M.B.A. and became a financial advisor. Bill always treated women with perfect respect, always deferring to what she wanted just like he did with the adult women in his life who raised him. He landed a good job with a medium sized firm earning a good salary, and that's when he met Karen. She was everything he ever wanted. He fawned over her, bought her expensive presents, and when she started hinting at marriage, he did the beachside proposal because that's what men are expected to do. Of course, Bill sought his mother's approval first, and she readily approved. Karen was his princess, and they would live happily ever after.

Or so he thought.

Bill and Karen were married when both were age 30, and there was no mention of those silly prenuptial agreements and protections in Bill's world. They were in love, they were looking forward to their happily ever after, and that was going to be enough. Over time, Bill and Karen had three children, and Karen stayed home with no thoughts of going back to work after giving birth to their firstborn, despite their agreement she would continue to work. Bill would never hint at asking Karen to do something she didn't want to do, so he just worked extra hours to make up the financial difference while his career progressed. According to Karen, this decision was eventually vindicated when Bill became a partner with his firm and the money started flowing in. Bill and Karen bought their dream house and dream cars, sent their kids to private school, and, with money inherited from his grandfather, Bill and Karen bought their dream vacation home at the beach. Happily ever after was progressing nicely.

Unfortunately, 15 years after being married Karen became bored once the kids became independent enough to get themselves up and ready for school, and so Karen started having an affair with her youngest son's soccer coach, Kyle. Bill put up with a lot from Karen, because, you know, "Happy Wife, Happy Life." But now poor Bill is divorced from Karen because the infidelity was a bridge too far, even though his own mother pleaded with him to forgive Karen. And his mother did so despite the fact that Karen was still screwing Kyle behind Bill's back. "You just need to try harder to win her back, dear," his mother told him.

In the divorce, here's what Bill lost (even though Karen is the one who cheated on Bill because it was a no-fault divorce state):

- He lost the house in its entirety;

- He lost half the vacation home that was paid for with grandpa's money because at the time he purchased it, he titled Karen's name jointly on the deed with him;

- He lost half of the investments he owned;

- He lost half of his 401k;

- Karen got the more expensive of the two cars;

- Bill pays alimony and child support; and

- Karen doesn't have to work until the youngest child turns 18, more than a decade away.

In less than a year, Karen went from being Bill's princess to the evil witch bent on making his life miserable. She even had the nerve to move Kyle into the house Bill paid for. Meanwhile, Bill is now living in a one-bedroom apartment with loud neighbors keeping him up at night, and he gets to see his kids every other weekend while hearing about all the horrible things that "Mommy said" about him and about all the great things Kyle did with them.

Welcome to modern America.

Unfortunately, this is something that happens all the time, and it's not just happening to men these days. It's happening to women who are the primary breadwinners in the family, but we'll get to that in a bit.

It doesn't have to be this way.

If you want to be the type of person, the type of man, who's going to end up securing themselves and their future for themselves and their kids, even at the expense of a wayward spouse who's going to try to take advantage of you when things turn bad, then we need to learn from poor Bill's mistakes and take a look at how things should be done instead. We need to know how to set up a divorce firewall between your future spouse and your hard-earned wealth.

Now here's the story of Rob Paulson. Rob was raised by a single father whose mother was not in the picture. His single father Dan taught him all of the lessons that he learned after seeing what his mother did to his father in a divorce. Dan intentionally raised Rob to have an independent streak, ambitious habits, and a strong work ethic. Rob learned many lessons from his father on the way men interact with others, not just women. He was always skeptical, especially of women who batted their eyelashes at him, and while he learned to appreciate the good things in life, he was never going to expect some princess to fall into his lap because she was "The One."

"Relationships are hard work," his father taught him. "People can change over time, and when they do, you may be the one losing out. So, appreciate those good times, but always protect yourself before any bad times come."

Just like poor Bill Peterson from the first story, Rob attended college where he majored in economics, went on to graduate school to get his M.B.A, and then became a financial advisor. Rob was working on his career and life, and women were just an occasional distraction for him. He valued and respected women for who and what they were, but Rob would never put a woman on a pedestal, and he never tolerated disrespect. Rob landed a good job with a medium sized firm earning a good salary early in his career, but eventually he started his own firm once he learned how to really make money at the financial advising game.

Rob was already set up with a protective trust as well as a series of corporate entities owning his major assets, such as real estate and cars. That's when Rob met Stacy. He was in his early-30s, and she was in her late 20s. Stacy was loyal, agreeable, and always made Rob feel like he was the most important man in the world. After a year, Stacy and Rob signed a cohabitation agreement and moved into one of the properties Rob owned through an LLC titled in the name of his trust. They also both signed a month-to-month lease and equally paid rent. Within a year, Stacy started talking about marriage, and that's when they had the talk about a premarital agreement.

After talking to her mother, Stacy said she wasn't fond of the idea, giving the usual arguments about how prenups were like expecting the marriage to fail. However, Rob flipped that argument on its head telling her that if the marriage was going to succeed anyway, then there would be no harm in creating and maintaining a premarital agreement… and if she didn't like it, then they could simply not get married and continue on the way they were or call it quits. It was her choice. Stacy changed her tune, and they both went to their attorneys to hammer out the details.

Rob was married to his wife when he was 35 and she was 30. They had three children and, 15 years later, Stacy cheated on Rob with a coworker. (The situation is sounding a little familiar, isn't it.) But fortunately for Rob, this story has a much better ending for him and for his kids. Here's what happened to Rob in the divorce:

- Rob kept the house since it was purchased by his trust, Stacy wasn't on the deed, and, in fact, Rob didn't even own the house directly for it to be even considered in a divorce;

- Rob kept the vacation house that was purchased with inherited money, because he put the money into his trust, and his trustee purchased the vacation home through a newly created LLC, and it even generated some rental income from time to time for the trust;

- Rob kept all of his investments since the excess money from his paycheck and distributions from his firm also went into the trust to purchase those investments;

- Rob kept all of his vehicles because all of them were owned through corporate entities in the trust;

- Rob kept his retirement and Stacy kept hers, because that's what was in the premarital agreement;

- Rob pays no alimony because that was also in the premarital agreement, and because Stacy agreed to not stop working (nor did she) and had her own income to support herself;

- Rob is paying some child support because he earns much more than his now ex-wife does, but he always knew that he would; and

- Rob and Stacy have equal joint custody because that is also what they agreed to in the premarital agreement, and the judge found no reason to alter that.

Rob is living a good life, he sees and raises his children half of the time, and the other half of the time he is working hard on his business or pursuing his own hobbies (with a few casual female friends on the side).

This can also be modern America. That is, if you're smart enough to deny the fantasies of finding "The One" and simply finding someone who is suited to be your spouse. You can still take all of the right legal precautions to make sure you do not get devastated in the event of a divorce while working to make sure that your marriage is not on the wrong side of the statistics. You can have a firewall strategy just like Rob did.

Getting "divorce raped" is a very common story among men. They hear it all the time from friends and family members, and they see the devastation that's wrought on them. This is despite the fact that everyone is always encouraged to marry for love, and they maintain this fantasy until the fantasy comes crashing down. But if you can keep your head about you, then you can prepare appropriately. And as we are in the 2020s and will soon be in the 2030s, we are seeing a lot more of an equalization of education and salaries among men and women. We're seeing a lot of women becoming the breadwinners in the family. More and more men are the ones giving up their jobs and staying at home to raise the children. And now when there's a divorce, we're starting to see the women being the ones paying alimony. And child support. And losing half their house and half their investments. And they do not like this at all. Nor should they.

This isn't a men versus women issue, nor a spouse versus spouse issue. It is an issue of protecting yourself as best you can in this world because no one else is going to do it for you.

If you're going to get married, then you need to make sure you're defending yourself appropriately in case things turn bad. This doesn't mean you are "dooming the marriage before it starts" by getting your ducks in a row, preparing legal paperwork, and executing legal agreements.

That's crazy. In divorce, you don't end up losing someone else's love and affection in a legal judgment. You don't end up losing the feeling of a partner's acceptance and love by virtue of a court order. You end up losing that anyway because the relationship is over. The court is all about finances and property, so if you want to legally protect yourself, and your finances, and your property, then you need some legally protective documents and to employ the right techniques. Be a lot more like Rob or you'll end up like Bill.

This book can show you how.

Chapter One:
Using This Book

One of the benefits of having an attorney that looked ahead long term was starting out a life strategy the right way. As soon as Rob Paulson landed his first real job, his father made him go to a planning attorney who understood business as well as estate planning. "Get used to meeting with a lawyer a few hours every year so you don't need to hire one for a hundred hours to clean up a mess," his father Dan told him.

Rob wasn't really sure why he was meeting with Chuck Ocean, Esq., but that's who his father recommended, so he went.

Over the course of an hour or so, they covered estate planning documents, discussed potential business entities should the need arise, and looked at investments. Then Chuck started asking him about his relationships. "Your father told me to discuss finances, lawsuits, and divorce with you, so we might as well," Chuck said. "Even if you don't have a relationship right now, there is a lot of value in getting things set up now, particularly a specialized trust that protects your assets, which can definitely be useful in the event you ever do decide to get married."

Rob rolled his eyes, shook his head, and sighed. He hated his father's lectures on the dangers of society, too much government interference, and particularly about how there are women out there trying to scam men. It always sounded so defeatist when Rob just wanted to be hopeful. Even more than he hated the lectures, Rob hated making mistakes that proved his father right. And his father was right a lot.

"OK," Rob started. "A lot of the things you've talked about have no application now, but tell me what I should be doing at this stage of my life and career."

As an attorney who built a law practice on providing education to my clients that helps them make smarter planning decisions, I would suggest reading every part of this book to soak up all of the information it contains in order to better protect your life and your savings. However, I acknowledge that not all of my clients want or need that much information in order to make the right planning decisions for them, and they are more interested in the "what" and "how" of the Divorce Firewall Strategy, but not the "why" explained in some of the chapters. That is why I have broken down a few different situational overviews with the accompanying chapters that would be most helpful.

Once you do start reading through those chapters and understand how different techniques can start to interact with each other, reading some of the additional chapters may be of increased value to you. The fact is, the more you have, the more you want to protect it from the perils of a potential divorce.

In this chapter, I have laid out three levels of wealth, but I hesitate to put firm numbers to any given level because your interpretation of what meets a certain level of "wealth" is more important, and so I have described the levels of wealth in more general terms. Therefore, I have only categorized them as starting to accumulate, having some wealth, and wealthy. In all of these situations, we are assuming you are not married, at least not yet.

Here are the situations:

Wealth Level 1: Starting to Accumulate

This is most people starting out. Perhaps you have obtained your education, you have been working a few years, and now that you are starting to feel more financially secure, you don't want to screw things up. At this point, you do not feel that if you were to retire today, you could at least live a comfortable life and you must continue on your financial grind.

Here are the chapters to start with:

- The Ideal Plan

- The Domestic Asset Protection Trust

- Cohabitation Agreements

- Premarital Agreements

At this stage, knowing this information can be critical to setting things up correctly before getting into a serious relationship, and making sure that you are protecting yourself. Having at least the Domestic Asset Protection Trust in place and accumulating more assets through it can be the cornerstone to a successful Divorce Firewall Strategy by the time you have a serious relationship. Coming back to this book and its other chapters can also be of great benefit to you down the road as you accumulate assets, particularly assets like real estate if you intend to rent it out.

Wealth Level 2: Having Some Wealth

At this level, many people have gotten a few promotions under their belt or have stabilized their own businesses, and they are starting to think about planning ahead for retirement. In other words, they are actually starting to project what it would take to live comfortably if they retire today, and they might be at or close to a point where they could liquidate everything and live a boring but comfortable life… as long as they aren't spending too much money on luxuries. Leaving the money they leave behind to their loved ones is on their mind, and they are serious about their estate planning. There may or may not be children at this point as well.

Here are the chapters to start with:

- The Ideal Plan

- The Domestic Asset Protection Trust

- Cohabitation Agreements

- Premarital Agreements

- Corporate Entities, Contracts, and Specific Assets

- Contracts, Leases, and Other Agreements

- Trusts and Other Legacy Planning Documents

- The Complete Divorce Firewall Strategy

While this constitutes most of the book, it still focuses a lot on the "whats" and "hows" rather than the "whys," but these additional chapters from Wealth Level 1 become important to managing the wealth you do have as well as discussing how to pass the wealth on to the people you want should you pass on.

Wealth Level 3: Wealthy

You have definitely made it, and you have enough to retire comfortably any time you want, but most likely you still want to stay active. Perhaps your business has reached the maturity level or you have a C-Suite job, and you probably have accumulated investments as well as real estate that is being put to work making you money. You definitely are thinking about the next generation and passing on wealth, and perhaps the main concern is making sure that if you leave your wealth to your children, or other family members, that you do so in a protected way so they don't lose it to divorce, lawsuits, or disability.

Here are the chapters to start with:

- Just read the whole book

If you have accumulated this much wealth, it is also important to understand why things are the way they are to help give you context. After all, there could be millions of dollars at stake, and understanding why you are taking these steps is worth the extra time it takes to read the whole book

As I already mentioned, this is an entire strategy, and multiple moving parts are necessary. With your hard work on building yourself and your wealth, you can utilize most or all of these techniques to keep yourself safe from a potential divorce.

Chapter Two:
The Law is Against You

Rob Paulson and Bill Peterson weren't exactly friends, but they were cordial enough. After all, they knew each other from their M.B.A. program, and it was a welcome coincidence when they ran into each other at the conference. After the lectures and workshops ended for the day, Rob and Bill decided to grab a drink at the hotel bar.

"So what are you working on right now?" Rob asked as he sipped his whiskey and Coke.

"This cute blonde named Karen," Bill replied with a smile, sipping his fruit-infused martini. "We've been dating for about six months now, and I think she's The One."

Rob involuntarily frowned but recovered, making it seem like it was the bite of the whiskey making him grimace. "I mean what are you doing to build yourself and your career?" Rob clarified. "I'm probably about a year from branching out on my own, and my attorney already has a trust set up for me and some business incorporation ideas. Are you doing anything on that end?"

"No," Bill said, smiling into his drink. "I'm actually happy working at my current firm, and in about three or four years I'd be in line for a junior partner position. Besides, I'm making enough now that between my and Karen's jobs, we're going to do well. The junior partner bump in pay is just going to be the icing on the cake."

"Have you talked to anyone about a prenup?" Rob suggested tentatively.

"Oh, no," Bill said laughing. "A prenup is just betting that the relationship is going to fail. We're not going to have one."

"Have you talked to your lawyer about this?" Rob asked.

"No, but I talked to the wisest person I know," Bill said. "My mother says the same thing, and she absolutely adores Karen. We don't need to have paperwork to know it's going to work out."

"Suit yourself," Rob said, knowing that conversation was at a close but not without one more comment. "My attorney already has my premarital agreement drafted on his computer, and I don't even have anyone in mind just yet. We'll just fill in the blank with her name, if and when I'm ready to propose."

They both had a laugh at that, but Bill would remember this conversation in the years to come... after the unthinkable happened.

While Bill Peterson's case is a fictional one, it has a lot of elements that happen all the time, every day, to men everywhere, and even more recently to women. What exactly is going on in divorce when it seems that the law is against you no matter where you turn? Let's get a good lay of the land for family law and see what is the norm right now, which is no-fault divorce.

What exactly is "no-fault divorce?" No fault divorce eliminates the need for any kind of reason to get divorced. It means you can get married, swear oaths to each other to remain true and faithful to each other, in sickness and in health, until death do you part. And then one day your spouse can decide they aren't happy enough, divorce you, get alimony and half of your assets. There is no need to prove any kind mistreatment, infidelity, or abandonment in order to get a divorce.

On the other hand, your spouse can cheat on you. They can neglect you. They can publicly disrespect, humiliate, and insult you, and none of those reasons matter in a divorce case (even though it may matter in child custody questions.) It just doesn't matter when it comes to whether or not a divorce happens, and how the finances are split up in no fault divorce states. (There is also a recent push in some states to bring back requiring some misconduct in order to get divorced, but why would anyone want to stay married to someone who doesn't want to be with them?)

With the advancement of the Internet, and particularly Reddit and YouTube, more and more men are seeing what is happening on a macro level, and they are refusing to get married in the first place. Divorce rates are staying consistent, but marriage rates are declining. It is also clear that when people are presented with other potential opportunities beyond their current relationship, there is a decent probability that they will explore those options. We are supposed to be in a society where everyone is equal, and men and women are equal with equal opportunity for success. At the same time, when married couples end up in a divorce court, the person with less ends up taking assets and income from the person who has more... even if they are the ones leaving the relationship. It seems like the law is against you, and it often is.

But still we move forward. As society progresses, women are provided equal or better opportunities to have financial success on their own. They are generating their own income and amassing their own wealth. We are in the age of The Strong, Independent Woman. Too bad government, divorce law, and the family court judges who make decisions have not caught up with this concept. Men are still considered to be the traditional "provider," men are still expected to support an ex-wife, men are expected to pay child support, and men are losing substantial assets in a divorce. Why? Because that's the way it is. It is built into the law, or more accurately, the people who execute the law.

That is, it's built into laws that also allow people, to some extent, govern their own relationships by having the right documents in place at the right time, but people rarely take advantage of them the right way. That is what this book is about.

We could just leave things there and move on with how men can protect themselves from losing everything in a divorce, but I believe it is important for the reader to understand throughout this book why government and the courts work the way they do. It is easy for frustrated men in bad positions to become jaded and believe that government, or even The Women's Movement, is somehow out to ruin them. That they are just out to punish men. That men are the enemy of women and the government.

That's simply not the case, and if you think about it logically, you'll see what is really going on.

- Government has limited money.

- Politicians who make the laws don't want to raise taxes to get more money if they can avoid it.

- When couples end up in a divorce, there is a much greater likelihood that the non-breadwinner in the relationship would end up taking government resources through food stamps, Medicaid health insurance, housing subsidies, and various children's programs.

- Rather than the government paying for food, shelter, and health care to the non-breadwinner after a divorce and getting those additional resources by raising taxes on everyone, government will let the breadwinner pay for these things. Even if it doesn't appear fundamentally fair to do so.

There is something else we need to consider: The topic of common law marriage is making a comeback, and at the time of this book being written several legislatures are at least discussing it while it is pretty much an established law in certain provinces of Canada while being called something else.

In the U.S., there are already eight common law marriage states:

- Colorado

- Iowa

- Kansas

- Montana

- New Hampshire

- South Carolina

- Texas

- Utah

Why are there discussions about common law marriage and at-fault divorces making a comeback in other states? Again, it's not to punish men for just living with a woman and not marrying her, or forcing unhappy, or even abusive, married couples to stay together. It's not to advance some moral agenda. It's because couples are starting to simply live together without marriage, maybe even have children, and then going their separate ways. Simple enough, right? Does the government really care about the fate of the people going their separate ways? Not really... except if the non-breadwinner is taking advantage of those state government resources and government can get someone else to pay.

Thinking that the government, women, or feminists are somehow out to punish men through the family courts is an emotional response by men like Bill Peterson, but it's not worthy of the Rob Paulsons of the world. While the information contained in this book can help you structure your life and assets in a way that can set up a divorce firewall and prevent "divorce rape," it is meaningless if you are more influenced by your emotions than logic. Following just your heart in relationships is like sheep following the shepherd into the slaughterhouse because they like the pleasant tune he's humming. If you can keep your head in life's driver's seat rather than your heart, you'll fare much better in life and relationships, and you can actually bend the law to your will.

If you know the rules when others don't, you can win the game.

☐

Chapter Three:
Bending the Law to Your Will

"Thanks for coming in," Chuck said to his client Rob and his cousin Rick, laying down his notepad on the broad conference room table. Rob had brough his cousin and best friend Rick to the attorney's office to review some protective planning in which Rick was going to play a role. However, Rick really didn't know what was going on, but he was going to help his cousin out no matter what.

"My pleasure," Rick said a little hesitantly. "I have to say, I'm really not sure what I need to do."

"That's what this meeting is all about," Rob answered before Chuck could.

"Exactly," Chuck said, looking to Rick. "We're in the process of setting up something called a Domestic Asset Protection Trust for your cousin, and he wants you to be the Trustee."

"You mean, Rob wants me to take over his trust if he dies?" Rick asked.

"No, we actually need you to be the trustee now in order to protect Rob's investments and future business," Chuck said. "You would actually be the person in charge of the trust even though Rob would really be managing the assets, including Rob's future business once it's formed. Through setting up the trust and assets the right way, Rob gets to decide the makeup, functioning, and running of the assets, but only you would be able to give Rob money or let him use his own assets for personal purposes. If we set things up the right way, and

more importantly run and manage things the right way, Rob's assets would be immune from lawsuits, particularly divorce should he ever get married, against these assets."

"How does that work?" Rick asked with a very confused look.

"The law and the courts are against people with money these days, particularly men with money when it comes to divorce from a woman without money," Chuck said evenly. "But there are specific rules, entities, and techniques in a wide range of legal areas that can be combined to bend the laws to your favor without breaking the law."

Rick settled back into his chair while Rob actually leaned forward on the table, knowing he was about to hear the good stories from his attorney once again. "Go on," Rick said.

There are certain areas of law where you can really bend the rules to fit your situation, your goals, and your objectives. It's not universal, but there are a lot of customization techniques you can use to make sure the law treats you, and your assets, the way you want rather than the way others or the government wants. For non-attorneys, it's amazing just how much you can structure the form and function of your own life and relationships, provided you do it the right way. The easiest area of law is the one that I've been working in for my whole career, and that's estate planning. When it comes to estate planning, you can basically do whatever you want with very few exceptions. This also consequently is where your parents can leave you an extremely protected legacy, and where you in turn can leave the next generation the fruits of your labor in a bulletproof way.

Unfortunately, very few people actually do this. This is why there are default areas of law where the law is just "taking its best guess" at what the average person would want. In North Carolina, the state I'm licensed as an attorney, if you die without a will then the spouse is NOT going to get everything but will instead split the estate with children, or your parents if there are no children. What if one of the kids is passed on? Their share goes to their descendants. And everything goes outright to beneficiaries at age eighteen. This isn't what most people want, but that's what the law states.

That is, that's what the law is if you are like most people who don't actually get off their assess and put together their own plan. If anybody tells you they don't have an estate plan, that's not true. They just have the state-sanctioned, government-approved estate plan because they didn't bother to create a Will or a Revocable Living Trust. You can pretty much do whatever you want, leave whatever assets you wish to whomever you wish, and as long as the plan is created and executed properly.

What are some of the exceptions to being able to do whatever you want in your own estate plan? Well, you can probably take 3 guesses, but my guess is you'll only going to need one: You can't disinherit a spouse. A spouse has to be a beneficiary of your estate plan up to a certain degree because the government has an interest in making sure that the spouse doesn't end up impoverished, just like we talked about in the last chapter with why the divorce courts go the way they do. But there is even more flexibility here because it's an elective right that the spouse can come forward and exercise if they wish. Basically, a spouse has to come forward with the right legal paperwork to say "Here I am! I'm demanding the amount that I'm allowed to get under the law! They can't exclude me!" Thing is they can be excluded because that "election" can be waived in a good premarital agreement. Once those rights are waived, you and a spouse do whatever estate plans you each want without including the other as a beneficiary.

What are some other areas of law where you can bend things to your will? Business contracts and leases can also be customized, but there are a lot more restrictions than with estate planning. There's more regulation because the government has an interest in making sure that people don't end utilizing government resources if things go poorly. For example, when it comes to renting and leasing property, there are a lot more regulations and restrictions in place when it comes to residential leases as opposed to business and commercial leases. Some of the more restrictive regulations in residential leases are:

- A minimum number of days of notice you have to provide someone before you can evict them. You can't just show up at the door and say, "It's my property, you've paid through today, so I want you out right now." If that were allowed to happen, then the person likely becomes homeless, they end up going to homeless shelters that may be subsidized by the government, and now the states have to pay because a paying tenant suddenly became homeless.

- There has to be a certain amount of security provided. Without living premises being even marginally secure, then people could be robbed quite easily, lose everything, and, again, become dependent on the government to survive.

- Minimum climate and comfort guidelines. While older generations may make it sound like people are spoiled by modern heating and air conditioning, it is actually vital to the economy that adequate housing be available to workers for industry to survive. This also applies to the support companies and workers in the area that cater to all workers, such as shopping, restaurants, and entertainment. Imagine what the Deep South would look like if air conditioning wasn't intentionally made available. Would it really have developed the way it did if they couldn't get skilled workers to move there because it was so uncomfortable? And would the governments in those states be getting the kind of tax revenue they are without those industries and workers?

While different states vary, having minimum restrictions doesn't mean the landlords and tenants can't negotiate more within those areas. Rent can be higher if other amenities are provided. If there is a minimum 30 days' notice for canceling a lease, both the landlord and tenant can agree to 60 days instead. There is more room for negotiation, and this would be considered more regulated than estates, but less than the next area of law, which is divorce and child support.

The government definitely doesn't want spouses to become impoverished, but, more than that, the government wants to make sure that children are supported. Not only is it expensive to raise dependent children, but it also looks bad if the government allows children to be neglected... but it's not the government's problem if they can make it your problem. In the event there's a marriage breakup and the kids end up in the middle being fought over, the mandatory child support guidelines in most states mandate that children be taken care of if they were produced during the marriage. This also applies through adoption and other ways of becoming a parent.

When looking at child support laws, it is becoming increasingly clear in a lot of states that there are legal formulas being used so support becomes very, very predictable. If the husband makes X amount of money and the wife makes half that amount of money, and it's 50/50 custody, then the husband's going to be paying money to the wife in the form of child support according to the formula until the child reaches a certain age, usually 18.

There is no negotiating child support down. There's no way to agree to either not pay at all or pay less. You just aren't going to get away with not paying the amount state law provides. And, in addition, you can be forced to pay more under most state laws if the spouse provides good enough reasons to demand more in court. Also, you better be paying the money to the court, because if you pay for eighteen years of child support according the amounts laid out in the guidelines, but you and the other parent decide to just pay cash directly, then the other parent can come back and claim you never paid child support.

Thing is, no matter what proof you have that you paid the money to the other parent, if it didn't go through the court then the judge will likely treat the payments as a "gift" and still order the payment of the "back child support."

Does this mean there is no way to address child support in a premarital agreement? Yes, there is. You can always agree ahead of time to pay more or pay beyond age 18. Like I mentioned, this area of law is extremely restrictive. But surely you and a spouse can agree that alimony and spousal support are off the table, right? Not completely.

Even with a solid premarital agreement, the state does not want a spouse to end up on food stamps, in public housing, and receiving welfare payments when there is someone else who can pay, meaning you. While it is often limited in duration, if a husband has all of the assets, all of the income, and a solid premarital agreement that states the spouses get nothing from each other, there is some support for the spouse leaving with nothing. There are two types of support:

- Post-Separation Support: One spouse pays the other spouse support payments until a final determination is made by the court, which may be based on both one spouse not being able to maintain their lifestyle and the other spouse having the ability to pay the support.

- "

- Rehabilitative" Alimony: One spouse pays the other spouse support payments in order to get them back into the workforce and re-establish their own lifestyle.

Depending on state law, these forms of support may be unavoidable. However, in a practical sense both forms of support are designed for non-working spouses suddenly being separated from their lifestyle to be able to maintain or regain their lifestyle. So, if you have a premarital agreement that states both spouses will continue to work, and you actually ensure that happens, then these forms of support are much less likely to be needed.

Even in this most restrictive area of law, if you have a solid premarital agreement, state clearly that both of you will continue to work, and then don't put up with it if your spouse suddenly decides they don't want to work, then there is some leeway in getting out of paying that type of support because it isn't needed.

When it comes to the financial aspects of family law, some things you can change, and other things you can't. But if you take a real hard look at it, the financial areas that can't be changed are because the government doesn't want to pay when you have the ability to. What exactly happened when we were talking about Bill Peterson and Rob Paulson? How were their cases so radically different? It's because Rob took advantage of bending the law to his will ahead of time. He had the right agreements in place, he enforced them, and he secured his own money and assets in just the right legal way. Rob understood the rules of the game and played it accordingly, so when he got divorced, he didn't lose the game the way Bill did.

Why did Bill lose so badly? Bill believed in the fantasy. Bill believed he found "The One," and that they were going to live happily ever after, so there were no legal steps taken to protect himself. When the divorce finally happened, Bill was blindsided. He didn't do anything to bend the law to his will ahead of time, and he ended up losing close to everything because of his rose-colored glasses.

In the next chapter, we're going to take a hard look at Rob Paulsen's plan and what he put together to make sure that he was protecting himself, as well as his kids, before marriage and well into the future.

Chapter Four:
The Ideal Plan

"This all sounds confusing," Rick said. *"There are so many moving parts to this."*

"There are," the attorney Chuck said. *"But each component has its own purpose, and once things are set up the right way, the most complicated thing to figure out is the taxes. And that's not your issue, it's the accountant's problem."*

"Rick, I'm sorry that this sounds like a lot, but it really isn't," Ron said. *"Like Chuck said, when you break it all down and lay out what each person is responsible for, you really don't have a ton to do."*

"For example, there's the Domestic Asset Protection Trust that will shelter all of Rob's assets," Chuck said. *"You would be the trustee in charge of deciding whether or not to distribute money or assets to Rob, so from time to time you would write a check. You would also be the person giving Rob permission to live on a property owned by the trust, and there would be some documents to sign there."*

"What about the running of the financial planning business you were talking about?" Rick asked, turning to Rob. *"What about the investment accounts you mentioned? What about those?"*

"That's the great part," Rob said to Rick. *"I get to be the Investment Advisor, so I handle all of that. You may have to sign some paperwork, but I'm the one really managing the assets while you're the person deciding whether or not I personally get money."*

"OK, maybe you should go over these components item by item," Rick said *while pulling out his notebook and a pen.*

In this book, we're going to explore different legal documents, techniques, and strategies to get you to an overall plan that can protect you from a marriage or other relationship gone bad so that your situation looks more like Rob Paulson's and not at all like Bill Peterson's. It's important to note that there are no miracle cures or cherry picking an item and thinking this one thing is a miracle cure to all relationship vulnerabilities. Let me give an example of one of these "miracle cures" happening around the time I am starting the writing on this book.

Soccer sensation Achraf Hakimi and his actress wife Hiba Abouk are embroiled in a divorce. When they arrived in court, though, Hakimi ended up shocking his wife by revealing that he owned nothing. Apparently, he had been consistently directing his salary and fortune to his mother so she could title the assets in her name rather than Hakimi accumulating it himself. All of the houses, apartments, and wealth were all owned by his mother, and if he wanted something, his mother would just buy it for him.

And suddenly everyone in YouTubeLand, social media, and other digital spheres were shouting about how everyone should now just put their assets into their mother's name as the ultimate, best, and sole way to protect against divorce with no need for any comprehensive strategy.

Unfortunately, this "duct tape" advice is as dangerous as it is simplistic, and it could lead to huge problems in some common circumstances.

- What if mom dies? Is she leaving everything back to you, or does her estate plan leave everything to all of her children? What kind of protection do you have at that point with the assets back in your individual name?

- What if mom is sued? Those assets are now on the chopping block for a big legal judgment.

- What if mom gets upset with you about something and decides to give your assets to other people?

- What if your mom says "no" about something important you need and are requesting money for?

All of these circumstances can and do happen in this world with great frequency, and if you have turned over your life's savings to someone else there is little you can do to get your assets back. What benefit is protecting 50% of your assets against a divorce if you simultaneously risk losing 100% just because the technique is simple? No, it will take a little more work and strategizing to get you to a high level of protection with a much lower risk of losing, but if you are the type of person who is driven to accumulating wealth through intelligence and hard work, you already understand that.

In this chapter, we'll review the legal documents and arrangements we'll flesh out in the remainder of the book, as well as a summary of some techniques and strategies. Think of these legal documents and arrangements as tools, and the techniques and strategies as ways to use the tools in a coordinated strategy like Rob Paulson did. Having a legal document is not enough just like having a wrench to fix a car is not enough if you don't use it properly.

Legal Documents and Arrangements

The Domestic Asset Protection Trust

A self-settled irrevocable trust can be the most powerful legal protection vehicle available against not only divorce, but also lawsuits, creditors, bankruptcy, and loss of disability and other public benefits should the need arise. Commonly called a Domestic Asset Protection Trust, it is created by the person who wants protection, they place the assets they want to protect into the trust, and they are the first-level beneficiary. This trust is not available in all states, but there are techniques available to have your trust and assets come under the jurisdiction of one of those states even if you live elsewhere. Other than a lot of formalities to make the trust work, the biggest drawback is that you can't be the trustee of the trust, nor can you distribute assets or money to yourself, so choosing the right trustee becomes a critical decision.

This is where Rob Paulson put most of his assets before and during the course of his marriage, and it is partly what protected his wealth from the divorce court. By not having any ownership or control over distributions from these assets and accounts, they weren't even eligible to be on the table for a divorce. This trust will be covered extensively in this book since a lot of the other techniques should be incorporating and referencing the trust as part of a coordinated strategy.

Cohabitation Agreement

Before living with someone you are in a romantic relationship with, it is vital to have a cohabitation agreement in case things do not work out, or even if the relationship does work out that the agreement is a defense against claims that the cohabitation was actually a common law marriage. The terms are very similar to a premarital agreement in that the document covers basic life and financial topics such as how expenses are shared, which assets are separate property, and which assets are clearly defined as jointly owned while everything else remain separate. Without a solid cohabitation agreement in place before moving in together, you are putting your assets at risk. This agreement in combination with other techniques can make your life and financial future far more secure, and we'll explore this document and the overall strategy in more detail.

Premarital Agreement

If after reading this book you still decide to get legal married, then at the very least put a solid premarital agreement in place to ensure that if the marriage dissolves you don't lose everything like Bill Peterson did. Unfortunately, most people often only find out just how much they can lose in a divorce after it happens to them, and then they shake their heads at their naivety and what they wish they knew before getting married. If they had a solid, well-crafted, and comprehensive premarital agreement (a prenup) which contained the right provisions and was periodically updated, then a lot of the different ways they lost out in a divorce could have been avoided or at least mitigated. But the premarital agreement is only one component of the overall protective marriage strategy we'll explore later.

Limited Liability Companies and Corporations

Having a corporation or limited liability company own real estate, cash, and other valuable investments can ensure that some high-value assets gain additional legal protection. More importantly, it solidifies the argument that the Domestic Asset Protection Trust comes under the chosen state laws if the entities are owned by the trust and are also incorporated/formed under the same state laws. Of course, the business entities actually have to actually act like a business in order to have corporate protection from lawsuits. For example, just titling a house in the name of a limited liability company but not having the trust rent it to you under a proper lease agreement where you are paying rent is just begging a court to let someone get through the protective shields you are trying to build.

Contracts, Waivers, and Other Agreements

What a wonderful world it would be if people kept their word and remembered things perfectly. But we know that is not reality. That's why there are contracts, leases, waivers, and other written agreements to avoid the pitfalls of faulty memory and outright lies if someone turns vindictive. However, depending on the phase of the relationship, the agreements don't necessarily have to be complex. If you are going to get into a romantic relationship to the point of spending the night at one another's places, it is also time to make absolutely sure there is documentation that clearly defines the relationship and living arrangements, even if it is as simple as stating you are not living together. While not quite as comprehensive as a cohabitation or premarital agreement, they can nonetheless be invaluable if there is a dispute.

Trusts and Other Estate Planning Documents

Many times, people look at trusts only as a way of planning for where your assets go after you die, but these and the usual complementary documents can be critical in the event of a health crisis as well as protecting your assets from being confiscated by a court in a domestic or legal proceeding and given to someone else. In particular, the Domestic Asset Protection Trust can be the keystone to an entire protective strategy that will also work in tandem with more traditional estate planning documents and techniques, even to the point of providing generational protection for your own children during their lifetimes so what you leave them will likewise not be lost to divorces or failed relationships. Having the right estate planning documents can make sure your wealth continues on to the people you want… and exclude people you don't, such as a spouse.

Techniques and Strategies

Keeping Property Titled Separately

One of the worst mistakes people make after getting married is titling their assets jointly, especially if only one person is putting all or most of the money into the account or asset. I can't count the number of stories I hear about a married couple where one spouse makes the entire down payment and makes all of the mortgage payments, but the house is jointly titled in the names of both spouses. In a divorce, it is extremely likely that the house would be split equally, and one spouse has to "buy out" the other spouse for half of the house's equity. If you intend to keep most assets separate, then do not start titling or retitling assets and accounts jointly.

Rigid Compliance with Agreements

A big reason legal agreements fail to do what they are supposed to do is people don't follow them. They assume that just having the agreement in place means if the crap hits the fan that they are protected. However, if you are acting in contravention to what is laid out in the agreement, then why should anyone, especially a court, force everyone else to honor the agreement? Probably the simplest example is something I see all the time in the small business world. Someone opens a small business, they file Articles of Incorporation to give their business corporate protection… and that's all they do. They use money from the corporate checking account to pay their personal mortgage, and they use money from their personal checking account to pay the business's utility bills. They never get around to drafting corporate bylaws, and having written minutes for their mandatory annual meetings is never done. When they eventually get sued for something that happened in the course of business, the attorneys end up going after all of the business and personal assets because they didn't actually treat their corporation like a separate entity. Again, there's a fallacy of convenience that simply having a document magically solves all of your problems, and it can be fatal to what you are trying to protect. And this is all on you for not following through. When you hear about "prenups don't work," there is a strong possibility it didn't work was because someone didn't actually do what they were obligated to do.

Rigid Enforcement of Agreements

The exact opposite of compliance with the agreement on your part is failing to enforce the terms of the agreement on the other person's part when the don't play buy the rules. The more you "let things slide" with a spouse or partner on what they are obliged to do under an agreement, the more wiggle room they have to put aside those terms in the agreement. Imagine a solid premarital agreement that states both spouses will continue to work, both spouses will continue to equally pay rent and utilities, and both spouses will equally contribute to the household chores. Now imagine that the wife decides she doesn't want to work anymore, she lounges around all day not doing any housework, and she also stops contributing to the expenses she's obligated to under the prenup. Instead of calling out the wife on her obligations, the husband just lets it go. He doesn't push her to get a job, he takes overpaying for all the rent and utilities, and he does all of the housework… for three years.

Do you really think a judge (a representative of the government) is going to enforce provisions in the prenup mandating no support or alimony be provided when husband took no steps to make his wife comply with the agreement, work, and financially contribute to the household? Especially if it means that now that she has been unemployed for three years and she would likely end up needing food stamps, Medicaid for her health insurance, and other welfare programs, is the judge going to put the financial burden on the State instead? Now imagine it was about three or four months instead of three years and she had been making false promises of trying to get a new job. A judge is now much less likely to throw out those terms of the agreement because you were trying to stick to the terms of what you both legally agreed to, she was only out of work for a short period of time and is still employable. Agreements give you rights and responsibilities, but you can't let the other party get away with not living up to the terms of the agreement.

Combining Relationship Agreements with Business

A strong potential technique in an overall strategy is combining obligations under a relationship agreement with your own business and trust operations. The best way to describe this is through an example I will repeat in different sections of the book. If you are in a relationship and have decided to cohabitate, then you should be putting together a cohabitation agreement with one the terms being that you will both equally pay towards rent. That's fair, right? But where will you live? There might be this nice condominium available for a reasonable rent that together you can both afford. The landlord is XYZ Property Investments, LLC, a Wyoming limited liability company doing business in whatever state you are living in. So, you both sign the lease, and you both equally pay the rent. However, XYZ Property Investments, LLC is actually owned by your Domestic Asset Protection Trust. In essence, you and your partner are paying all of the rent towards a condominium that you actually own, so you are pocketing their half of the rent and paying yourself the other half. Of course, there are other terms that need to be incorporated into the lease, and it is up to you if you are going to disclose this arrangement in a cohabitation agreement (depending on the state you are living in and the advice of a family law attorney), but you certainly should under a premarital agreement.

Documentation

This should go without saying, but I have come across problems with this so often as an attorney with more than 27 years of experience with my clients that it needs to be highlighted. You need to document everything, including keeping well-organized records and accessibility to the legal documents and agreements. You need to make sure that documents are executed with multiple originals, an original set is accessible to you and another set with your attorney, the documents are scanned, and the scans kept on file where you can get to them, and assets and accounts and routinely checked and collated. It is astounding how many of my clients from the earlier years of my practice who kept both sets of estate planning document originals have their children come forward years later looking for the legal documents... and the clients managed to lose both sets of originals. This can be as simple as a locked cabinet or fireproof safe with the documents and flash drives regularly updated and stored.

Tax Professionals Who "Get It"

One critical factor I'll keep mentioning along with these strategies relates to taxes, and that you need to have a good tax professional who understands not only taxes but the goals and objectives of the overall strategy. There are simple tax preparers who handle simple 1040 returns. There are accountants who understand more complex personal situation, or accountants who focus on small business owners, or accountants who understand both. Then there are also accountants who will understand the ins and outs of revocable and irrevocable trusts. However, one very common problem with all of these professionals is tax myopia; no matter what you provide them, they'll always try to persuade you to act in a way that makes you pay less in taxes above anything else.

While that sounds good on the surface, it can be deadly to asset protection techniques like the ones we are discussing here.

For example, it is customary for accountants to try to shelter money from year to year in IRAs, 401ks, and other tax deferred accounts because it lowers your overall income tax liability for that year. However, tax-deferred retirement accounts are not allowed to be placed into trusts and keep that tax status, and it has to remain in your individual name. If it remains in your individual name, then there is always a possibility that half (or more) of it could be lost in a divorce. What amount of tax savings is worth a risk of losing half of your retirement?

What you will really need for the types of strategies we'll be covering is an accountant who understands trusts, businesses, and above all is not so focused on the tax aspect that they lose sight of the overall protective strategy. They need to be willing to sacrifice some tax savings, maybe even what they would consider significant tax savings, to keeping your savings protected. If an accountant becomes that focused on taxes to the point they are willing to sacrifice the asset protection strategy, then simply ask if there is a potential, unproven, and risky tax deduction potentially saving 10% on your taxes that year that they would be willing to recommend if it meant you have a 50% chance of losing half your life's savings in an audit. I doubt they would make that recommendation.

Maintenance, Maintenance, Maintenance

Unlike getting married, these legal arrangements aren't simply done once, and all of the legalities are automatically maintained over time. Imagine going to divorce court 20 years after getting married and trying to tell the judge that you shouldn't really be held to the marriage laws because it was so long ago, situations changed, your spouse wasn't the same loving person they were when you got married, and now the marriage vows "went stale" and should just be set aside. Sounds crazy, doesn't it? However, that is precisely what a divorce attorney would argue for their client if they wanted to get them out of abiding by the terms of a premarital agreement, and it just might work. When it comes to all of these arrangements, especially cohabitation and premarital agreements, they need to be maintained and even renewed periodically. Now imagine an attorney trying to argue the same thing in a twenty-year marriage when the premarital agreement was updated six times with each party having their own attorneys review the updated agreements before signature. It's difficult to simply argue that the premarital agreement "went stale" when it was just a few years earlier that it was reviewed, renegotiated, and signed.

There is no one document or technique that is going to provide you with ultimate, ironclad protection. But the right combination of legal documents, techniques, and the discipline to stick to the rules can provide you the best protection possible under the law. In the next few chapters, we will review the main documents and protective techniques using our good friend Rob Paulson as an example.

Chapter Five:
The Domestic Asset Protection Trust

"This isn't right!" The short, blonde woman stood up and screamed to the room. "He's hiding money from me and the court! It's not right!"

Rob Paulson sat and shook his head, following his attorney's advice to keep quiet and let him do the talking. It was a much larger conference room in a different office than Rob was in when he and his soon-to-be-ex-wife Stacy signed the original premarital agreement more than fifteen years ago, and an office once more removed than the one in which he and his cousin Rick signed the Domestic Asset Protection Trust a few years before that. But it was still with Rob's same attorney Chuck Ocean, and the new divorce attorney Stacy hired since the one who assisted her all these years told her something she didn't want to hear. Since signing the original trust, Rob has been systematically and intentionally putting all of his investment money into that trust in order to shelter it against lawsuits, bankruptcy, creditors, disability... and for this very moment that he wished never happened.

"Tom, please control your client," Chuck said in an even tone. "Screaming doesn't accomplish anything."

The other attorney in the room looked at Stacy, and she sat down with a huff. Obviously, he had already spoken to Stacy about outbursts, and she didn't like being restrained at all. This was a very different Stacy than Rob new, previously loved, and married fifteen years ago. Then again, the Stacy he married fifteen years ago would never have cheated on him either.

"Now, Chuck, what my client is saying is true, isn't it?" Tom replied, looking at every face the room, including Rob's cousin Rick who sat fuming with his arms crossed. Rob sometimes thought that Rick was even more upset with Stacy than he was, and it was Rob that Stacy cheated on and started the divorce process.

"No, it's not true," Chuck replied. "Nothing has been hidden since the terms of the premarital agreement, and the four updates to it over the years, all reference that Rob had this trust and that it would forever remain his separate property in the event of divorce. Your client signed that original agreement and all four updates, and she had her own attorney to represent her. She always knew it was there."

"But I didn't know he would keep putting all of his money in it!" Stacy shouted again.

"But you did know that Rob's excess money was his to do with as he pleased," Chuck said while squarely looking at Tom. "You did agree in all five versions of the agreement over the years that he could spend, buy, or transfer his money to wherever he wanted, and you would never have part of that money in the event of divorce."

"I've been spending all of my own money, so all I have is my rental property!" Stacy said in exasperation, but then turning a little snotty. "That's not going to keep me in the lifestyle I've grown accustomed to."

She definitely got that phrase from one of her divorced friends. Probably Francine who took her poor shell-of-a-man husband to the cleaners.

"What your client did with her money was always up to her," Chuck said before Rob could say something back. "The fact that she spent her money rather than saving it is her problem. The premarital agreement says they each could do what they wanted with their own earnings, and my client decided to keep it in his protective trust."

"How much money is in the trust?" Tom asked, looking down at some papers.

"None of your business," Chuck replied.

"How much money is in that trust?" Tom now asked Rick directly. "You're the trustee. How much is in there?"

"Get bent," Rick replied, his arms remaining folded and a grin appearing on his face.

Well, he didn't actually use the words "get bent."

The story of Bill Peterson versus Rob Paulson and what happened in their lives with the divorce really highlights how planning ahead can save you from bad divorce outcomes. One of the big components in Rob's firewall plan was the Domestic Asset Protection Trust.

These highly specialized trusts are not your average, run-of-the-mill estate planning trusts, such as a revocable living trust. Those trusts have their own value in estate planning, and they can be highly effective in protecting your assets for your heirs after you are gone. But they are not designed for *your own* asset protection. With a revocable living trust, you maintain complete control, power, and authority over your own assets, and therefore you also have the same personal liability you had over those assets without the trust. In the case of the Domestic Asset Protection Trusts, they are highly protective, irrevocable trusts that have to be set up in just the right way under specific state laws, because not all states allow them.

There are currently 17 states that allow Domestic Asset Protection Trusts, and those are Alaska, Delaware, Hawaii, Michigan, Mississippi, Missouri, Nevada, New Hampshire, OH, Oklahoma, Rhode Island, South Dakota, Tennessee, Utah, Virginia, West Virginia and Wyoming.

I haven't done a complete comparison off which state is best, but the research I have done shows that they all have advantages in many areas but some drawbacks. For example, a Wyoming domestic asset protection trust requires you to have a minimum personal liability insurance policy for a million dollars, or for the complete value of the assets in the trust, whichever is less. The trusts that I will primarily be referring to are situated in Wyoming in most in this book, mainly because, as you'll read later, there is a national way to get access to these valuable trusts, even though you can always go directly to an attorney located in the specific state you wish that allows Domestic Asset Protection Trusts.

Some important discussion points are:

- State ties to bring the trust under the protective state laws
- The roles of the Trustor, Grantor, Beneficiary, and Trustee(s)
- Retained Powers
- Choosing Trustees
- The Discretionary Trustee
- Investment Management
- Contributions
- Distributions (or not)
- Interaction with trust assets

Ties to the State

One critical item with domestic asset protection trusts is that you have to have some specific ties to the state that you want it to have jurisdiction. For example with Wyoming's laws, there has to be at least one trustee who is tied to that specific state who is physically present, they are authorized to do business in those states, and it's either an individual resident or some other professional, banking institution, or a Trust Company chartered under that state law, or at least authorized to conduct business in Wyoming. The trustee should also have a physical office branch in the state in order to meet the corporate trustee requirement.

There are some other conditions required to have the trust fall under the various state laws and provide the protection. Often there have to be assets in that particular state. It doesn't necessarily mean real estate, or having substantially all of the assets located there, but often having some level of assets in bank accounts or investments inside that particular state is enough to fulfill that state's jurisdiction requirement.

Here's an example of doing it poorly, and it's similar to situations I often see when people are trying a do-it-yourself approach to setting up corporations and the business owner simply files Articles of Incorporation with the state with nothing more. The business owner thinks that one act is all they need to do in order to get corporate protection under their state's laws. That just doesn't work. You need bylaws, shares of stock issued along with stock certificates, a corporate record book, and there has to be written annual meeting minutes for shareholders and the board of directors. Without those formalities, it is very likely that a lawsuit will get through the personal protection that normally exists with corporations, and now the person or business suing you can get to your personal assets.

When it comes to a Wyoming Domestic Asset Protection Trust, the poor example would be signing the trust document, but locating all of the assets in New York, having all of your trustees located in New York, and never purchasing the mandatory personal liability insurance policy required under Wyoming law (if it is a "spendthrift trust"). If the case ends up in a New York divorce court, there is a good chance the judge will set aside the trust since it didn't comply with the Wyoming laws it was supposedly set up under, and they won't allow the protections normally afforded Domestic Asset Protection Trusts under Wyoming state law.

So what requirements are typical when we're specifically talking about Wyoming? There are actually two specific types of Domestic Asset Protection Trusts in Wyoming with different requirements. Yes, you do have to actually execute the trust document under Wyoming state law in all cases, but you also need some other provisions depending on whether the trust is a spendthrift or discretionary trust.

For a Spendthrift Trust, meaning the trustee is required to provide you with basic necessities out of principal and income, the trust must contain the following provisions to be valid (along with other trustee requirements mentioned later):

- The trust must state that it is a "qualified spendthrift trust" under § 4-10-510 of Wyoming statutes;
- Be irrevocable;
- Expressly state Wyoming law governs the validity, construction, and administration of the trust;
- Contain a spendthrift clause that restricts the beneficiary from demanding income and principal beyond what is necessary for their health, education, maintenance, and support;
- The settlor (the trustor and grantor) must have personal liability insurance equal to lesser of $1,000,000 or the value of the trust assets;

The second version, which I prefer, is a discretionary trust, meaning the trustee has complete discretion to provide you funds or not. The reason I prefer this version is that it also potentially ends up locking up the assets for public benefit programs purposes, such as Medicaid paying for nursing home care five years after you transferred the assets in. It also has far fewer requirements under Wyoming state law (again with a few more trustee requirements referenced later):

- Provide for discretionary distributions of trust income and/or principal to the settlor; and
- The trust must be governed by Wyoming Law.

These are just some of the basic requirements to bring the trust under the jurisdiction of Wyoming. But there are also some other features of the trust that will have some Wyoming requirements, particularly with regard to trustee powers.

Trustor, Grantor, Settlor, Beneficiary, and Trustee

There needs to be a trustor, who is the person setting up the trust, and a grantor placing the assets into the trust. These two roles are often combined into the term "settlor." In this case, that has to be you, the person setting up the trust. And there needs to be a beneficiary, which also has to be you. *You* have to be the person who is setting up an establishing this trust to protect you and protect your assets as well as being the beneficiary, most likely the only beneficiary in place for this particular kind of trust.

Sounds like you are in complete charge of the trust so far, right? Well, in order to get all of this protection from a marriage falling apart (or from lawsuits, creditors, bankruptcy, and disability) you cannot be a trustee with the ability to distribute that money to yourself. So now suddenly there's this wall that's put up between you and your own assets. The trustee has to be able to give you money or not, and they have to have that ability to say no to you. A lot of people come across that point and don't like losing control. However, this is a situation where you need to be separated from control of your own assets in order to gain all of the protections we are talking about.

When speaking about irrevocable trusts to my clients, I often refer to The Godfather Part II. There is a scene in the movie when Al Pacino's character Don Michael Corleone is in a Senate hearing. There is a big board with all of the names of the various bosses, captains, and other members of the crime family arranged in a hierarchy, but there is no direct tie to Michael whom they placed at the top of the chart. However, everyone watching the movie knows that even though Michael Corleone is not officially giving orders throughout the organization that he is the person in charge, and the benefits of the organization are his to enjoy. You need to think of yourself as the Don of your trust, even though you are not the person actually and officially giving orders.

We have been talking generally about a Trustee, but the fact is that the overall duties of the trustee can be broken out over a few trustees, and in these types of trusts that is often the case. While the distributions of income or principal is in the hands of a trustee, to come under Wyoming law there must be at least some powers and responsibilities in the hands of a Wyoming trustee, regardless of whether it is a spendthrift or discretionary trust. A Wyoming trustee must:

- maintain custody of some or all of trust assets in state;
- maintains records (can be nonexclusive, meaning records can also be located elsewhere in addition to Wyoming);
- prepares or arranges for the preparation of income tax returns;
- or otherwise materially participate in the administration of the trust.

As you can see, these requirements are not great so the majority of the trust administration can still be handled by a trustee outside of Wyoming. In general, I have been drafting trusts so just the required duties of a Wyoming-based Trustee are handled by such a person or company, and they are labeled the "Administrative Trustee." This way, the conditions of the law are met to keep this a Wyoming trust, but the more important powers and authority can rest with another Trustee regardless of where they are located. Who should handle these other trustee roles, particularly who will decide whether or not to distribute assets and money to you?

Retained Powers

As the Settlor/Grantor/Trustor, you have to give up a lot of control over your own property and investments to make the Domestic Asset Protection Trust work, but there are usually some significant powers you get to keep. For a Wyoming trust, you get to keep:

- The power to veto distributions, which is important if something comes up where you can't have money "in your pocket";
- An inter vivos or testamentary general or limited power of appointment which allows you to direct where the assets go after you die;
- The power to add or remove a trustee, trust protector, or trust advisor, which gives you the authority to fire someone you don't believe is looking out for your best interests and replace them with someone who will; and
- The power to serve as an investment advisor to the trust so you can manage trust assets even if it doesn't give you the authority to make distributions.

As you can see, there are still a lot of safeguards built into the Domestic Asset Protection Trust for you to ensure that things run smoothly according to your own strategic plans while still keeping the firewall up between you and the painful financial effects of a bad divorce.

Discretionary Trustees

There are some limitations on who you can choose to be a trustee in charge, but it really needs to be someone that you trust to look out for your own best interests as the trustee. They do have a fiduciary duty to look out for you, but at the same time you still want someone who is going to basically give you what you want when you want. The reason for giving the trustee such broad discretion on whether or not to give you assets is so that no court can force you to make the trustee give you money that can be lost in the divorce or lawsuit. There are always ways to remove the trustee if they're not actually looking out for your best interests, since you are the beneficiary, but they have to have that discretion to distribute assets to you or not in order to get the protection.

Who exactly should be your trustee when you're putting together a Domestic Asset Protection Trust? The first hard and fast rule should go without saying since trust is primarily to protect you in the event of a divorce, so your spouse should *never* be the trustee. Another restriction typical in all irrevocable trusts is that the beneficiary can't name spouses, children, parents, or siblings who are by default "subordinate" to you and your wishes. This also includes employees or others financially dependent on you so there is no way that you can threaten their livelihood if they don't provide you with distributions on demand.

There is some leeway we've seen with siblings, but this is admittedly a little bit of a gray area. The Treasury regulations talk about siblings as being subordinate, but siblings fight, argue, and disagree all the time. If there's enough potential information, documentation, and other evidence to show that a sibling is independent of you enough, then they may be able to be trustee. On this, I would at least check specifically with the attorney who's helping you set this up in a particular state or jurisdiction to get the pros and cons. However, there's nothing preventing you from naming your best friend as the trustee who's going to be making these discretionary distributions or not.

Investment Management

In a lot of cases, even though you are not allowed to be the Trustee, you can hang on to the management functions of assets within the trust in several ways. Depending on state law, you can specifically be the "Investment Advisor" or "Investment Manager" who is determining the makeup of the trust investments, which assets to purchase, sell, or exchange… although even as a "trustee" you cannot distribute money or assets to yourself. This is specifically allowed under Wyoming state law. A different and safer way to look at this overall is that the trustee can allow you to be the Investment Advisor with authority to make those particular transactions under the terms of the trust, although to avoid any potential for someone to challenge the trust stating you maintained too much control it should be explicit that you are not allowed to distribute assets in any way, shape or form. Safer still if the particular state law you want your trust to be controlled by is vague, then the trustee can retain all of those powers, meet with you about your investment wishes, and create and sign the paperwork themselves.

The second way that you're maintaining some control is if part of these assets is also inside corporate entities, then you can still manage the entities as a corporate officer, or if it's an LLC as the manager. You can maintain control over the corporate assets that way, so even if you have a business set up that is held inside the Domestic Asset Protection Trust, while you can continue to run that business, it's just technically the stock or the corporate interests are owned in the Trust.

Contributions to the Trust

Another important factor is contributions. In a lot of cases with the Domestic Asset Protection Trust, you have to be the only one who contributing the assets to the trust under state law. I sometimes hear "My parents want to leave me an inheritance to me through my Domestic Asset Protection Trust." In general, that is probably not a good idea, and I'll review alternatives when we get to the section on estate planning, but there are different, better options for estate planning that other family members can use in order to leave you a protected inheritance without mingling assets that could violate the state rules of your own trust. After all, as you'll see in that same section on estate planning, you should be leaving your estate to your beneficiaries in their own separate trusts and not just turning over this Domestic Asset Protection Trust to them.

Beneficiary Distributions (or Not)

But by and large, most of the time when people are putting money into a domestic asset protection trust for market investments, real estate purchases, or other non-liquid assets that you want to be able to enjoy. If you're putting a personal residence into the trust that you are going to use, you can live in that house with the permission of the trustee. If it's a rental property, most likely you would put that property inside a limited liability company or corporation, and then if you and trustee agree, you can run and manage that rental property. You can even draw a salary from the businesses if that's what works to your advantage.

If you're putting after tax investments into the Domestic Asset Protection Trust, it's supposed to be there for long term accrual, not for short term emergencies. There's no real need to get to those liquid assets unless there is a big emergency, and those big emergencies should not be happening all the time. In those cases, the Trustee can assist you. Plus, you can and should still keep *some* assets of your own outside the Domestic Asset Protection Trust, even if it is not a large amount. But if this is to be a solid plan that's going to work and protect you not just from divorce, but also from lawsuits, creditors, bankruptcy and even disability, then the majority of your assets should be placed inside the Domestic Asset Protection Trust over time.

Here is what you absolutely should NOT do: You find a house you want to buy, so you approach the trustee and ask them for the money to buy it. They give it to you, and then you purchase the house and title the deed in your own name. Worse still, maybe you title it in your and your spouse's name as "tenancy by the entirety," which is the legal verbiage for "joint with a right of survivorship" for married couples. Now you have absolutely destroyed the protections that the Domestic Asset Protection Trust usually affords you. Instead, these big purchases can and should always be made into the trust.

You and your spouse could get the exact same benefits of living in the dream house while the trust owns it and without putting the house at risk by titling the deed in your name, or, God forbid, in both your names.

Interaction with Trust Assets

The Domestic Asset Protection Trust owns the assets titled in its name, and there is an independent trustee overseeing these assets for the benefit of the beneficiary. However, the trustee has to utilize the trust assets for your benefit, and, at least in Wyoming, you can retain the right to be the Investment Advisor for the trust overseeing the makeup and function of the trust assets. This also includes buying and selling assets, changing the makeup of stock portfolios, and running companies in the trust. Some assets are in business to make money, and others are there for your benefit to use. Let's take a look at a few examples of how interaction with different types of trust assets can occur with you as both the beneficiary and Investment Advisor:

- _Rental Property LLC_: The first house you purchased was eventually paid off around the time you set up your Wyoming Domestic Asset Management Trust, but when you decided to purchase a new house, instead of selling the old house you instead put it into a Wyoming limited liability company and then transferred the LLC shares into the trust. Who runs the LLC? When creating the LLC, you assigned yourself to be the Manager of the LLC even though the Member (the owner/controlling person in charge of the company, is the Independent Trustee acting on behalf of the Trust. So, you can still look after the property, screen potential tenants, and enter into leasing contracts with the chosen tenants on behalf of the LLC even though the trust owns all of the LLC interests. All of the profits flow through to the Trust.

- *Motorcycle Dealership in a Corporation*: Perhaps your passion is riding and repairing motorcycles, and you decided to buy a dealership with an in-house repair shop. Instead of owning it in your own name, you form a corporation (because that's what your accountant advised) and have the corporation own the dealership. But who owns the stock? If you transfer the stock into your Domestic Asset Protection Trust, then the Independent Trustee represents the stock on behalf of the trust. However, you can be appointed chair of the board by the Independent Trustee, and the bylaws and meeting minutes can reflect you also being the president, secretary, and treasurer of the corporation. You can basically run everything about the business, and even determine your own salary. However, all profits from the company flow through to the Trust as the owner.

- *Investment Portfolio*: Most people want to diversify their personal assets to include stocks, bonds, mutual funds, and brokerage accounts outside of their retirement accounts, and these securities can be placed into the trust. As the Investment Advisor, you can be empowered to buy, sell, trade, and otherwise oversee the entire portfolio. However, one thing you can't do is give dividends or money from liquidated stocks to yourself since the owner is still the Trust, so the Independent Trustee would need to approve any funds being distributed to you as an individual.

- *Personal Residence*: In terms of protecting yourself from lawsuits, divorce, creditors, and other vulnerabilities, keeping your home safe is often a top priority. After all, how many divorced men (and women) have you heard complain about "losing their home in the divorce?" I'm sure you've heard a lot of stories. If your home is owned by the Domestic Asset Protection Trust, then as the beneficiary you are allowed to live in the house with the permission of the Independent Trustee. And later in the book we'll discuss how you might even be able to lease the house to yourself and a partner/spouse, split the rent between the two of you, and earn some money. So not only could you protect your house from being lost in a divorce, but you can also earn some money along the way.

As you can see, there is still a lot of control you keep in different roles as the beneficiary, the Investment Advisor, and through corporate management positions. In later chapters on specific assets and techniques, we'll discuss in much more detail how you can maximize protection while enjoying and controlling some of these assets.

Chapter Six:
Cohabitation Agreements

"What do you mean?" Cassie asked, genuinely curious.

Rick had been in a relationship with his girlfriend for a little more than a year, and she was pushing to take their relationship a step further by moving in together. They had been spending the night at each other's places. Over the last few months, the 24 year old Cassie was starting to complain about the expenses she was paying at her place when she spent about eighty percent of the time at Rick's. While Rick didn't really have any objections to moving in together, at 30 years old and having been the trustee of his cousin's trust for a few years now, he learned to be more cautious when it came to financial entanglements with people in general. Getting together and signing a lease was something he wasn't willing to do without legal protection.

"A Cohabitation Agreement," Rick repeated. "Look, we're moving in together to see if this relationship works at the next level, right?"

"Yes, that's the plan," Cassie said, leaning against the counter and winking seductively at Rick.

"OK, be serious for a minute," Rick said, which was the usual response he gave when his girlfriend wanted to flirt herself out of a serious discussion. "We have agreed to find a little bigger place, split the rent and other expenses down the middle, and keep all of our other accounts and items separate, right?"

"Yes," Cassie said, straightening up and being serious. "All expenses right down the middle."

"Good," Rick said. "Then we should do this the right way by putting it in writing and making sure at the same time that if it doesn't work out once we do move in that no one is being stuck with bills for a place they aren't even living at anymore."

"How would we manage to do that?" Cassie asked.

"I think my cousin Rob has a place we can look at, and I'm sure he can make the rent affordable so even once person could afford it if it came down to it," Rick said. "Although I'm sure moving in together going to work out just fine. This way we can both afford something great together but still start putting our own money away each month."

You hear the stories all the time. A couple decides to live together, they hunt for apartments, and then they sign a joint lease based on what together they can afford. Their fantasy of taking this big step in a romantic relationship has a high probability of failure, but they don't plan for that. Four months into a year-long lease, she gets ticked off at her boyfriend, cheats on him with one of his friends, and he dumps her cold.

Now what happens? What happens to the rest of the lease? What happens to the joint bank account? What happens to the utilities in both person's names, or, worse, one person's name? If neither one can afford the lease on their own or neither wants to move out, do they just keep bringing random strangers to the apartment for drunken hookups? Just how unbearable can it get?

From the stories I have heard, it can get extremely unbearable to the point of violence, and that is in no one's best interests. So how do you prevent this from happening, or more to the point, how do you protect yourself if the relationship sours and the person you want to live with turns bad?

The answer is to not only have a solid cohabitation agreement, but to follow it in the best way possible.

Too many times, people confuse premarital and cohabitation agreements, and this is understandable since they both protect your financial assets in the event of a breakup, but there are some critical distinctions:

- It is a romantic relationship, but it isn't an agreement in contemplation of marriage;

- There are a lot of terms about keeping not just finances but lives separate; and

- Specific terms are included that forbid both parties from making it even appear that they are married.

In this sense, it is almost an anti-premarital agreement simply because it is partially designed to make sure you don't fall into an unwitting marriage or marriage-like relationship, particularly in a common law marriage state. A few years ago, a wealthy businessman in Canada was dragged into court and forced to pay alimony to a woman he never married. The Internet, particularly the men, screamed bloody murder because they kept all of their assets separate, and she even had her own apartment. He ran the entire arrangement by his lawyer, and thought he was safe. "They were just dating!" was the war cry from the men claiming that the government was out to get them just because they were men.

But that was not the whole story. This wealthy businessman made a few huge mistakes that I'm sure he never ran by his attorney:

- While she had her own apartment, it was rare that they spent nights apart;

- He asked her to quit her job so she could focus full-time on supporting his home life;

- He gave her a wedding and engagement ring; and...;

- He kept telling everyone they were married.

Yeah, it was no wonder he got tagged with alimony because they ended up fitting pretty well into the definition of common law marriage under the Canadian province's laws. I don't know which is worse for protecting your own assets; the thorough way this businessman ruined things by acting completely contrary to being unmarried; or the fools who download a fill-in prenup, scribble in the blanks with crayon, get married, and then cry foul when a judge throws it out fifteen years later.

For all intents and purposes, they were cohabitating together, and if this businessman had created a solid co-habitation agreement and followed it, he might not be paying tens of thousands of dollars a month in alimony. So, what terms need to be in a solid cohabitation agreement?

Necessary Cohabitation Agreement Terms

There are several vital terms that need to be in a solid cohabitation agreement. At first blush, a lot of these will look familiar when you get to the chapter on the premarital agreement, but they definitely need to be crafted differently. In addition, premarital agreements also allow for a lot of potential future co-mingling of finances and assets which, except possibly for a checking account for monthly household expenses, should be strictly off-limits with someone you are simply living with.

Preamble Terms: One of the initial sections of many legal agreements is a "preamble" that clearly states the intentions of the parties. In the strictest of legal interpretations, the preamble is usually not considered critical to a contract because it rarely states anything specific enough to be legally enforceable. However, stating very clearly that this agreement is 1) not in contemplation of marriage, 2) there is no duty for either person to support the other, and 3) that the rest of the terms are to be interpreted in light of the fact that the parties are rejecting marriage, and this means that the preamble enhances the terms of the agreement that could lead a judge to conclude that, yes, you really did mean to remain single and not share your assets or income.

Lease Terms: How should the lease be established, and what terms should it have? This might be the most controversial item when compared to how things are traditionally done. The lease should only be held in the name of the person who would keep the property should there be a breakup. This flies in the face of what most couples do standard when deciding to move in together since they will typically look for, and be talked into, finding a place expensive enough that they both can afford rather than actually keeping expenses low. However, planning ahead means making sure that should the relationship not last that one person can afford the lease on their own, including utilities and extras.

The Cohabitation Agreement should then describe how the rent is to be paid each month with the full cost being paid by the person who holds the lease and the other person giving them the money for their share of the rent. Why do it this way and not just have the other person pay their share to the rental company directly? Because handling the rent this way also diminishes the ability of the person not on the lease to argue that they were on the lease de facto since they have a history of checks paying rent.

Finally, it should be plainly spelled out that should the relationship dissolve that the other person has a reasonable time to move out and find a place of their own that complies with state law. For example, in North Carolina a person with no lease can be evicted in seven days, so this should also be the length of time the other person has to move out, and those terms should be in the agreement as well. (We'll cover this more in the chapter Contracts, Leases, and Other Agreements).

Gifts and Bequests: One of the terms of the cohabitation agreement that are also found in the premarital agreement is that the parties are allowed to make gifts to each other, and that anything contributed towards the running of the household or to the other person that isn't expressly written in the agreement is to be considered a gift. Why? This specific term is included so that a vindictive ex can't win in court arguing that their house cleaning or appliance repairs constituted reimbursable labor they need to be compensated for, especially if it is not their name on the lease.

Separate Property and Income Terms: It is vital to note that all separate accounts, real estate, and other assets of any kind that are separate property of one person or the other, and will remain separate along with any gains, income, and other growth on those assets. With a nonmarital relationship, this should go without saying, but when it comes to breakups, it could be easy for an aggrieved person to claim that you promised to divide an account with them. Having it in writing cuts off that argument to a great extent.

This is also a good place to reinforce that all income belongs to the person earning it, and that under no circumstances shall either party have any kind of claim or entitlement to the income of the other person. While this is usually more of a term in a premarital agreement, it doesn't hurt to also make this clear in a cohabitation agreement.

Jointly Owned Property: While it is common for married couples to have an account or two for the operating of the household, this should not be done with unmarried couples cohabitating together. If you do happen to get a joint checking account for household expenses or emergencies, then how this account is divided upon a breakup should be explained in detail, including allowing one person to simply take half and transfer it to their own separate account upon the breakup. And never, ever, ever keep more money in this account that you are personally OK losing. The need for a joint account for people cohabitating has been greatly diminished by the invention of Venmo and other money transfer applications, and arguments that you need to have this common pool of money really falls flat. It is best to simply not do it and keep all of your items separate.

Utilities and Subscriptions: Ideally, all utilities should be in one person's name, and that should be the person on the lease. In the event of a breakup, the person on the lease can simply carry on without interruption. This also prevents a vindictive ex from spitefully canceling service on necessary utilities after a breakup. However, when it comes to portable subscription services such as entertainment streaming, food shipment, and other delivery services, then it doesn't really matter whose name is on the account since the services can be canceled immediately. And in the event of a break up, any login and password information should be changed immediately anyway.

__Dividing Expenses__: Now we are getting to the heart of the financial aspects of the Cohabitation Agreement, and you are determining how all of these living expenses are to be handled. If all of the expenses are to be evenly divided, then it is simply a matter of keeping track of all expenses and following a simple mathematical process (with an example):

1. Add all of the expenses up, for example coming to $4,000;

2. Divide by two to get each person's share, which in this example is $2,000;

3. Do a quick calculation to see who paid less than $2,000 that month;

4. Subtract the amount they did pay from $2,000, so if they did pay $1,200 of the expenses already, then that leaves $800; and

5. That is the amount they should pay the other person that month

It is vital that this process be handled religiously each and every month at the same time because it is very easy for one person to push this off. While not pointing fingers at any one gender, it has been a very traditional and now outdated attitude that a man takes care of his woman. Therefore, it is much more likely that a woman may start to slip into those old norms and put off paying because they want to "feel taken care of." That can't be allowed to start even once or it could become an argument that "this is the way it should be." At that point, it becomes easy to simply keep paying more, and that could be fatal if the breakup ends up in court. Picking a specific day each month to review these expenses makes sense, and it should be put on the calendar, ideally at the same time you have a monthly budget meeting, which brings us to…

__Monthly Budget Meetings__: While it is important to divide the expenses at the end of the month, it is also important to look at the month ahead and behind in terms of larger expenses. You should both be providing input on needed purchases in the future, but you should also discuss any larger, last minute purchases that occurred in the previous month and what you thought about them. In the agreement, you should specifically have a dollar figure in mind about how much you should each be allowed to spend on discretionary household expenses that they want to get divided at the end of the month.

For example, if there is a $100 cap on discretionary household expenses without getting approval from the other person, then this avoids one person purchasing a $700 air fryer/blender and trying to pass it off as being "for the apartment." That said, there are going to be larger expenses that come up, and these should be discussed at this monthly meeting so they can be planned for and money saved to afford them so large "emergency" purchases should be a rare thing. On the other hand, these monthly budget meetings should make it clear that if one person really wants the expensive air fryer/blender that they can spend their own money on it and discuss whether or not the other person can use it.

While a lot of this sounds like it could devolve into petty arguments over money, it has been said that living together should be a "test run" for marriage. So if you think the monthly budget meetings end up being unreasonable fights over minutia, it is not likely to get any better in marriage and you should reconsider the whole experiment of living together.

**Household Chores**: Handling a household is not an easy task, and part of the reason you may be moving in together is to make life easier on both of you. However, there are a lot of "masculine" and "feminine" tasks that society still imposes on certain genders. "You're the man, you should be taking out the garbage and handling home repairs," or "you're the woman, so you should be doing all of the laundry and the cooking." In the modern world where everyone is equal, those gender stereotypes are no longer universally applicable, and a Cohabitation Agreement should be explicit about the division of chores.

Putting a lot of thought and discussion into this section will probably do more to provide a peaceful living situation even more than staying on top of the agreed upon finances. This is why a big brainstorming and discussion session can help put into writing what each of you is expected to do. For example, I grew up with my grandfather cooking most Sunday dinners because he spent some time in a second job as a cook in a top Italian restaurant, and he taught me some things. I also spent several years and summers working at a chain restaurant at the local mall. When it comes to cooking, I'm going to cook my own food because I know exactly how to make the food I want the way I want it, and I'm not going to rely on anyone else to cook for me. If I were putting together this type of agreement, I wouldn't default to the woman in my relationship doing the cooking, and I'm happy to share what I cook. When it comes to laundry, I have always been independent enough to do my own laundry, but I don't necessarily like it, so I'm not going to do anyone else's laundry and would be happy to give up that chore to someone else. These are items that should be negotiated, assigned, and then drafted into the Cohabitation Agreement so everyone is on board.

Other Terms and Techniques

There are several other items of note that should be kept in mind even though they are not being put into the actual Cohabitation Agreement:

- Just like with a premarital agreement, each of you should have your own attorney, the agreement should be reviewed and update every few years, and you should always be prepared to walk away if the agreement is not being followed. (There is more on these items in the chapter on premarital agreements.)

- Only lease an apartment that one person can afford on their own, particularly the person whose name is om the lease.

- If you are utilizing the Divorce Firewall Strategy of owning the property in a limited liability company, which is in turn owned by your domestic asset protection trust, then you should be named on the lease, and the length of the lease should be month to month.

- If the lease is through another real estate company or landlord, then consider the other person being the only one on the lease so you can simply walk away if the situation deteriorates and the relationship ends. Again, it is in the best interests of everyone involved that the other person can afford the lease on their own if it came down to it.

Another point that deserves a little more elaboration than a bullet point is "don't be a dick, but don't be a doormat either." In other words, it is important to make sure both of you stick to the terms of the cohabitation agreement, but you shouldn't be so rigid that you become a nightmare to live with. If you put a $50 cap on household expenditures in the Cohabitation Agreement, and your partner finds a $49 coffee maker to replace the old one that was breaking down, don't flip your lid because the sales tax made the purchase come out to $52.16. That would be the "being a dick" part, in case you weren't sure. However, if your partner had casually mentioned wanting a new refrigerator, you replied that you would talk about it at next month's budget meeting, and they go out and buy a $1,800 refrigerator that is 20% off, then just accepting that would make you a doormat. As with everything in a Cohabitation Agreement, including negotiating it in the first place, you can have firm boundaries but have a little flexibility when it comes to things you don't truly care about.

Chapter Seven:
The Premarital Agreement

"I can't believe it's already been five years since we last met up at this same conference," Bill Peterson said to Rob Paulson while sipping his same chocolate martini once again. *"Time flies."*

"I know," Rob replied, gently shaking his Whiskey Sour from side to side to mix it up a little bit. *"Things are certainly different for me. My own business is now in it's third year, the money is rolling in, and I finally decided to get serious with a woman. How about you?"*

"Oh, I did land that same love of my life I mentioned all those years ago," Bill said. *"Karen and I are now married for three years with one kid and one on the way."*

"How about work?" Rob asked. *"Did you ever get that promotion you mentioned?"*

"Next year," Bill said, looking down into his drink. *"Karen wanted me to spend more time at home while she was pregnant with our first, and that set the promotion back a year or two. But look at you, actually presenting at the conference this year. That's amazing."*

"Thanks," Rob replied. *"Being on my grind these past five years has made all the difference. And now that Stacy and I have started living together, she's already looking forward to getting married. I told her it's at least going to be a few years, and we're definitely doing a premarital agreement."*

"That again," Bill laughed. "You're actually going to make her sign a prenup? Karen would have slapped me if I asked her to do that."

Now it was Rob's turn to laugh. He gave a light chuckle and took a sip of his drink. Rob had seen hundreds of guys just like Bill since he started his financial services career, and there have been too many times he had to fill out a mountain of paperwork to split up one spouse's investment accounts. For those clients, it was always the same old story. Man marries woman, woman decides to stop working after having kids, woman decides to divorce, and now man has to lose half of the account he had been contributing to for years. Thing is, more recently it had been more than a few breadwinner wives having to give up half of their accounts, and they were not happy at all. If any of them had the same solid prenup that his attorney Chuck already had drafted on his computer should Rob ever marry, they would have been saved all of that loss.

Rob also knew there was nothing he could say to Bill in this regard. He had his mind set just as so many other clueless and hopeful saps did who didn't protect themselves ahead of time, and there was a fifty-fifty chance that Bill would become just another divorce statistic and another sad story.

"Here's to not becoming a statistic," Rob said raising his glass in a toast to Bill.

"Here's hoping your girl is The One," Bill toasted in return.

Ten years later, they would know who was right.

The premarital agreement, or "prenup" is the marriage protection document that most people know about. However, it is not the end-all and be-all of protection from divorce, and many people incorrectly create, execute, and maintain a premarital agreement to their detriment. Unfortunately, they don't realize just how badly they failed to protect themselves with this document until they get slammed in court and lose in the divorce. In this chapter, we'll review why prenups fail, the necessary premarital agreement terms, and how to maintain a prenup over time.

Why Prenups Fail

"Prenups don't work!" the YouTuber practically screamed into the microphone, lamenting the downfall of men everywhere whose fortunes were being stolen from their gold-digging exes. [Insert eyeroll here.] "A man works for years, decides to marry a woman, and insists on a prenup. They sign one, and then she leaves taking half his stuff because the prenup means nothing!"

As an attorney, I have an ingrained way of thinking about situations that was baked into me throughout law school. It's something I can't turn off, and many good attorneys will tell you the same thing. In law school, you are pushed to objectively analyze a situation, review the different legal principles in your mind, and tick off the pros and cons, and come to a conclusion. This happens automatically in my mind without prompting, and it applies in all situations for me, not just work. The next step in this imposed way of thinking is that when you actually have a client in front of you, you automatically reexamine that whole process trying to advocate for the points that favor the client and downplay, excuse, or dismiss the points that don't.

The YouTuber is screaming into the void because he is doing none of this, and the added problem is a lot of other people may be listening to the screaming because they want to feel like they aren't the only ones in a failed relationship who lost out in a divorce. (And it doesn't matter if its men or women since everyone feels like they lost in a divorce.) He's responding emotionally without a real, objective examination of the legal principles. Premarital agreements can be done successfully, and you probably won't hear about it on YouTube when it does. Why not? Because, like I said, even with a successful premarital agreement in a divorce, no one is ever thrilled with the outcome of their divorce. Think of having to change a flat tire on an empty road but you have a good spare tire, the jack, and even wipes to clean up afterwards; you're relieved you got the tire changed, but you're not thrilled because you had to change the tire in the first place.

So why do some premarital agreements fail, and how do you make sure a premarital agreement in your situation doesn't fail? Here are the top seven reasons prenups fail.

Not Having the Agreement in Writing: This sounds fundamental, but make sure your premarital agreement is in writing and signed. While most people would think of this, and certainly any attorney whose law license is worth the paper it was printed on, you need to have a premarital agreement comply with state law, and this always means that it must be in writing. Don't let a quick Google search for "agreements" let you think that just because your state allows legally enforceable verbal agreements that this applies to prenups. All 50 states require premarital agreements to be in writing, but some states do allow other kinds of verbal contracts to be enforced. The reason all prenups have to be in writing is that people under the pressure of a divorce have a huge incentive to lie, and while there are going to be legal proceedings in a divorce at least the terms of this contract would be in writing. Speaking of pressures and incentives…

Prenup Signed Too Close to the Wedding: One of the most effective arguments in getting a premarital agreement thrown out is that it was signed under duress, and a common "duress" factor is that the spouse sprung the agreement at the last minute. The argument goes that they were now caught with already having spent a lot of time and money on the wedding, the social pressure of needing to follow through with the wedding now that the wedding date was so near, and not wanting to have wasted a lot of time in their relationship to walk away if a prenup was not what they wanted. And this is a convincing argument that frequently works the closer the idea is presented to a wedding date. If a prenup is what you want prior to marriage, it is probably best to bring up the subject even before getting engaged or at least several months before the wedding.

Not Being Represented by an Attorney: When someone isn't represented by an attorney in putting together a premarital agreement, then they can always claim later that they didn't really understand the terms of the agreement. Depending on the different terms, that may very well be true. For instance, if a couple roughly makes the same income and they have a very balanced premarital agreement that lets everyone keep all of the accounts they bring into the marriage, all assets accumulated by the parties during the marriage are to be split evenly with no spousal support, and no one will be required to stop working, then not being represented by an attorney is not going to have a huge effect on whether or not the agreement is thrown out. However, if one party makes a lot more money and owns the house and other major assets, the other party is being required to not work and be a homemaker, and the agreement states that in the event of a divorce the parties keep all of their respective assets and there is to be no support, then there very likely would be an issue with the spouse who is staying at home not being represented by an attorney. This is compounded greatly if the other spouse earning all of the money and keeping their assets was represented by an attorney.

Not Owning Assets in Line with the Agreement: Part of a well-crafted and effective premarital agreement is a complete and honest disclosure of assets from both parties, at least to the point both parties legitimately sign off that they are satisfied with the disclosure, and nothing has been hidden. Another part of assets in the prenup is how assets are to be owned and titled moving forward during the marriage. If certain accounts are to be kept separate, then they need to be kept separate. If there are supposed to be certain joint accounts, then they should be titled in both spouse's names.

One common clause in most premarital agreements that keep situations flexible is that the parties can agree to retitle or create new assets and accounts jointly, and often such accounts would be divided equally. The mistakes come when life changes things, assets get converted or changed, and things are retitled incorrectly. Switching financial advisors and they set up separate accounts jointly or convince the couple to have joint investments because their management fees would be lower. A new house is purchased with one spouse's separate assets, and the real estate attorney assumes the house should be titled jointly as a married couple. Or more nefariously one spouse starts the paperwork to move or convert an individual asset of the other spouse, and the new asset or account suddenly becomes joint.

Not living in line with the agreement: Many premarital agreements aren't just about assets but also about income and lifestyle. The agreement may specify what assets each spouse gets to keep in the event of a divorce, but it can and often will detail how joint and individual living expenses will be paid. When the spouses roughly earn the same amount of money, then expenses will often be equal. If one party earns much more than the other, then expenses may be paid in proportion to income. Problems can occur if a party begins paying more for these expenses despite what the agreement states over a longer period of time. If that happens, it becomes easier for a court to put aside at least those expense proportions and award some support to the other spouse. By far, the better option is to either stick to the agreement or update the prenup to reflect the changed circumstances. Which brings us to the next big mistake…

Not Updating/Renewing the Agreement Periodically: Another way for a premarital agreement to be thrown out is for it to "grow stale" with wildly changed circumstances (or at least a judge buying when one party argues it). A premarital agreement done fifteen or twenty years ago and never affirmed or updated stands a good chance of a judge throwing it out and going with state law and rules instead. It is a good policy at least every five years, if not more often, to revisit the premarital agreement, with each spouse again having their own attorney, to review and then update or change the terms to reflect the current situation. This also includes updating the list of separate and joint assets, addressing new issues that may not have been addressed in the previous version (such as childcare and inheritances), and any changes in support terms. It becomes extremely difficult for a court to throw out a premarital agreement because it was "stale" when it is updated and signed every 3-5 years.

The Prenup is a Deficient Document (i.e., DIY): We saved the best for last, which is also one that is most likely to have YouTubers screaming about how prenups don't work… when a party downloads a template, attempts to do it themselves, and screws up something big. While it might seem easy to simply grab an online document, fill in a few blanks, and say "viola! it's a prenup," it's not that easy. Premarital agreements should be handled by experienced attorneys who know what to look for, what to include, what to exclude, and what to avoid. All it takes is that one simple misstep by a do-it-yourselfer to throw an agreement into turmoil and have it end up being thrown out by a judge in a divorce.

While premarital agreements need to include various terms in a balanced manner under state law, these seven factors can destroy the intent of the agreement. Putting together a prenup also isn't as simple as signing the document and then going about life. It requires that your life take note and comply with the agreement you both created, and, just like marriage, that takes a little work.

These are actions and items that will prevent a premarital agreement from working well. What items should be included in a premarital agreement to make it the strongest possible in case of a divorce?

Necessary Prenup Terms

There are several vital terms that need to be incorporated into a well-drafted premarital agreement before the marriage, and then again when it is updated from time to time.

Income and Contribution Terms: The agreement should have the basic terms that each spouse gets to keep their own income separately irrespective of what the other spouse earn. The corollary to this is that each spouse will contribute to the household expenses, and that is typically where some customization comes in. In contributing to the joint household account, the contributions can be:

1. *Equal Amounts*: This works if you have largely equal incomes, so you can determine how much needs to be contributed to the joint account monthly, and then you are both contributing 50% of that amount each month. For example, if you set the initial household budget income at $5,000 per month, then you will each contribute $2,500. (Of course, this number may have a way for you to agree to raise the budget amount while keeping the method of determining how much spouse contributes consistent.)

2. *Proportionately*: If you have largely different incomes, then it may make more sense to contribute in proportion to your incomes. For example, if the household expenses are $5,000 per month, you earn $20,000 per month but your spouse earns $10,000 per month, then since you earn twice as much, you would contribute two-thirds of the amount or $3,333.33, and your spouse would contribute one-third or $1,666.67.

3. *Percentage of Income*: There can also contributions based on the percentage of income which will then dictate how your household expenses should work out. For example, having each of you contribute thirty-five percent of your income to the household income would mean that $3,500 of your $10,000 monthly income goes into the joint account, and $1,750 of their $5,000 monthly income also goes into the joint account. This means that the monthly budget is $5,250, and it goes up or down depending on changes in your income.

4. *Mixed*: There can be some combination of these techniques. For example, you can both decide that you will each contribute to the first $4,000 per month equally, but then contribute an additional percentage based on income. If your income is $10,000 per month, and your spouse's income is $5,000 per month, you will both contribute the first $1,500 and then twenty percent of your income over that amount, then you would contribute ($10,000 minus $1,500=$8,500; $8,500 x 20%=$1,700) a total of $3,200, and your spouse would contribute ($5,000 minus $1,500=$3,500; $3,500 x 20%=$700) for a total of $2,200, meaning overall you are both contributing a total of $5,400 toward the monthly account.

The important factors here are that everyone is on the same page as far as what is contributed, how that number may change depending on changes to income and other factors, and that there are ways to address changes when there is an impasse. For example, if your spouse loses their job and finds one that pays significantly less, then there needs to either be an adjustment in the way you are contributing, or there needs to be a reduction in lifestyle. One thing you should never do is simply pick up the slack. This is how a spouse becomes dependent on you and your finances, and that dependency can lead a court to have you support them more than the premarital agreement originally anticipated.

The other main income terms that should be standard in the premarital agreement are that neither is obligated to contribute more, that contributing more in the future does not imply an obligation to continue to contribute more, and that neither party in the event of a divorce or separation will have any claim on the income of the other.

Separate Property Terms: It is vital to note that all separate accounts, real estate, and other assets of any kind that are separate property of one person or the other will remain their separate property. Another critical part of this declaration is that all gains, income, and other growth will also remain the separate property of that individual and such gains won't be looked at as "marital growth" in assets.

For example, if Husband owns a vacation property that is worth $200,000 at the time of the agreement, but then seven years later there is a divorce and the property is worth $400,000, if there are no terms about the growth of the assets remaining with the individual, then it wouldn't be surprising if the spouse tries to claim that half of the $200,000 in growth would belong to them since it grew in value during the course of the marriage. They can also claim that they helped contribute to the growth in value through repairs, overseeing renovations, or some other efforts. It has to be

For more information, go to www.DivorceFirewall.com

made clear that any contributions, repairs, or maintenance are to be considered gifted efforts that are not to be compensated nor gains shared.

The easiest way to think of and explain this from a stereotypical male point of view is if a husband or boyfriend performs some car maintenance for their girlfriend or wife that they are not expected to be compensated as a mechanic or given some of the sales proceeds if the car is sold. In this same way, any "improvements" by a spouse to your property or assets that you or you both may both be enjoying should not be looked at as compensable work nor eligible for sharing profits if the asset is sold.

Separate Property Listing: A listing of all separate property for each person should be listed along with current exact balances as of a referenced date. This is a critical part of the agreement where everything needs to both be disclosed while being listed as the separate property of each party. By listing everything honestly and accurately, and then simultaneously listing everything disclosed as being separate property, it comes under the protection of the premarital agreement and its terms.

Another option that I don't recommend is that the parties can waive the disclosure of assets and values because then there could be claims later that you "verbally lied" to them and it could be used as a basis for overturning the agreement. In my legal practice, I often help families protect their wealth when mom or dad needs long term care (i.e., nursing home care) by rearranging and converting their assets within the rules so that the government program Medicaid will take over and pay the nursing home bills. I often get sly grins from the family with statements like "well, I can just take the money out of the bank and bury it in the backyard… who's going to know?"

Medicaid will know. They absolutely will. They'll find the bank withdrawals, inquire about the money taken out, and then deny the Medicaid application assuming the money was simply buried in the back yard.

It is exactly the same with your assets when it comes to a divorce proceeding, especially when the assets are significant. And the greater the potential payoff, the better the private investigator who is getting paid to nail you to a wall. It is always better to disclose the assets and therefore prevent the spouse from coming back later and claiming that you hid or did not disclose assets. Not to mention the potential perjury, fraud, and contempt of court penalties you may be facing.

As part of this disclosure, the assets in the Domestic Asset Protection Trust may or not be disclosed depending specifically on legal advice from an attorney in the state or jurisdiction the premarital agreement is being established in. But here are some factors to keep in mind:

- If you are going to use the strategy of having the Domestic Asset Protection Trust hold a limited liability company that owns property you are leasing, and therefore putting you own money back into the trust, then it is likely to raise eyebrows from your intended spouse and their attorney if you are going to have your spouse pay part of the rent as a strategy mentioned previously. Raised eyebrows doesn't mean it shouldn't be tried, and those negotiations are up to you and your attorney.

- The disclosure can be as detailed or general as the parties agree. It's not completely out of line to simply list that there is an irrevocable trust which you are the beneficiary of but not the trustee nor having the ability to make the trustee give you assets, and just the overall value of the assets in the trust. There is nothing compelling you to list all of the assets in the trust as long as the attorneys and the potential spouse are not insisting on it.

- It is also potentially possible that the fact that there is an irrevocable trust which you are the beneficiary of without control to take money out that will be listed without disclosing the actual value. If this is the course taken, discuss with your attorney that it should also be noted in that disclosure that the potential spouse has been advised by counsel that the value of the trust was specifically not disclosed, and counsel agreed to that term.

- It needs to be noted that you can and likely will contribute more to this trust in the future. This way, there are no surprises like there was in the case of soccer player Achraf Hakimi and his wife Hiba Abouk. At the time this is being written, those divorce proceedings are still developing, but it would not surprise me if the divorce court counted all of Hakimi's salary and other income as being his for purposes of the divorce because he didn't disclose the arrangements to his wife. By revealing that more money is likely to be contributed to this trust over time in the premarital agreement, it eliminates the argument that you were "hiding" money during the marriage.

__Cooperation Terms__: One of those inconvenient things that pop up all of the time in the financial world is the presumption that your spouse has rights to assets and property just because you are married. A clause that must be in the premarital agreement is that you will both cooperate with each other in keeping assets separate now and in the future. For example, there are some businesses and government agencies that mandate that a spouse MUST be the primary pay on death beneficiary for all retirement accounts unless they waive their rights to be the beneficiary. This clause forces them to comply with signing the paperwork that waives that right to your 401k, 403b, or other employer-sponsored retirement plan or be in breach of the agreement. (And if they are not cooperating, then it might be time to readdress whether or not you should be married).

__Release of Marital Rights__: The cooperation terms are meant to address waivers in private finance and employment. However, there are also default marriage rights and responsibilities under the law that are also precisely what you want to avoid. There needs to be a solid statement about how this agreement is meant to release all of those terms (except what is mandatory under law). This is often a broad statement accompanied by a few "including but not limited to" terms such as rejecting alimony, spousal support, and equitable distribution of property that is deemed separate by this agreement. As discussed previously, there may be no way to waive emergency spousal support under state law, and there is certainly no way to waive child support.

__Gifts and Bequests__: One of the terms of the premarital agreement that needs to be explained is that the parties are allowed to make gifts to each other and that those gifts are not considered to be separate property. In addition to that, the language of these provisions should be clear when transactions are NOT gifts to the spouse. For example, purchasing a vacation property in a favorite destination of your soon-to-be spouse but titling the property in your own name (or better still in the name of the Domestic Asset Protection Trust) is not to be considered any kind of a wedding gift or a joint asset of the couple, and that it should be considered a separate asset of yours or your trust.

__Jointly Owned Property__: It is common for married couples doing their best to keep everything possible separate to also have a few accounts or assets that are owned jointly by both of them. The best example is the joint checking account where they have agreed to place their required contributions towards household expenses as explained in the section on income contributions. These accounts never usually accumulate much since accumulation isn't the purpose, and it certainly never accumulates so much that it would hurt you financially if it were all taken away in a divorce. There can even be terms about a maximum balance where the excess is distributed back either equally or in proportion to the income contributions method.

Many times, even couples who have premarital agreements may jointly own a house with a joint mortgage. Financially, if you are trying to build up your own wealth and can possibly handle the purchase of the house on your own, then do so. However, if the house is going to be a joint asset, then the terms of dividing the house upon a divorce must be clearly explained. This includes who gets to keep the house and how any equity is divided, and if there is a mortgage, then there also needs to be a clause about refinancing the house solely in the name of the spouse keeping it. By far, the better option is for you to own your own house through your Domestic Asset Protection Trust owning the LLC holding the deed to the house, and then both spouses jointly paying monthly rent.

Spousal Support Terms: The premarital agreement must contain the spousal support terms that you agree to, which really should be that there is no support either way, except for what is unavoidable according to state law. This clause also typically states that both parties are capable of working, earning income, and supporting themselves, and that they intend to maintain that standard after language.

Income Tax Returns: For federal and state taxes, there are two main choices regarding the filing of income taxes. The first and most popular is "married filing jointly," which is the option most accountants will tell you is appropriate. You can also be married but file separately, but this often means higher income taxes since filing jointly may mean more deductions. However, this also means your spouse can get access to your returns and see the whole picture of what is in the trust. Keeping your trust income and earning private may override the concerns you have about any specific deductions, but you should make sure to weigh the different options before committing to either. I'm sure there are also other options, but these should be discussed with your accountant to make sure you chart the best course.

For more information, go to www.DivorceFirewall.com

**Waiver of Rights to Retirement Accounts and Income**: One of the biggest vulnerabilities you can have in a divorce is a spouse getting some of your retirement through the court process. There is actually little you can do to protect retirement accounts from the spouse through trusts, corporate structures or other means without losing the tax-deferred status other than having solid provisions in the premarital agreement. Therefore, other than actually limiting the amount you put into your own retirement accounts, this is one doubly critical section in a premarital agreement because there are no other secondary protections. In addition, while pensions are a rarity these days, if you are actually going to potentially draw a pension from your work or your own company or companies, then this section should also be crystal clear that a spouse has no claim on your pension.

**Employment and Work**: Just as important as making sure your assets and income are not to be confiscated in a divorce is making it clear that there shouldn't be a need for your assets and income to go to a divorcing spouse because they can't support themselves. This section needs to clearly state the following:

1. That both of you are employed/self-employed;

2. Where you are employed and what your current salaries are;

3. That neither of you is requesting the other to not work, and that both of you intend to work throughout the marriage until retirement;

4. If there are brief periods of unemployment because of children being born, that such periods are limited to a maximum maternity/paternity leave time frame you both establish which will be shorter if such time frame is established by your respective employers, and then you both must return to work at that time; and

5. What happens during periods of voluntary and involuntary unemployment.

Shit happens, and people can become involuntarily unemployed. I saw a lot of my clients and their children go through periods of massive layoffs in 2000 and 2008. This section should clearly lay out that during periods of involuntary unemployment that there is a certain period of time that the other spouse has to get a job, how many months their contributions to the household can be abated but paid back later, how unemployment benefits should be applied for, and what happens to the family budget during those times.

Sometimes there are also solid reasons for quitting a job, but in those cases consider not allowing any abatement of that spouse's contributions to the joint account. If they hate their job and want to quit, then they should be saving extra over several months in order to be more secure when they quit, or they should begin looking for a new job while still employed. In either voluntary or involuntary unemployment, there have been far too many men getting stuck paying all the bills for up to a year or more because their wife just decided to quit and their husband was "too understanding" towards their wife and let her continue to spend household money and the husband's discretionary money without contributing. I have heard to many stories and seen too many situations where a wife wants to simply not work because her friends have been telling her that since her husband makes so much money that she shouldn't have to work. And, yes, this definitely does happen to wives with husbands who give up, but they usually spend days on end playing video games and not getting out to look for a job. Neither situation should be tolerated.

Realize that these terms may sound harsh to a spouse, but when we get to the section on enforcement of the agreement, you'll see that you can be strict without being a jerk.

Alimony and Support: Other critical terms in every premarital agreement reference alimony and support, specifically that there should be none, or if there is that the amount, type, and duration of support is definitively laid out and explained. As mentioned previously in the book, there may be some types of support that can not be avoided in the case of emergencies. But beyond those specific emergency situations, the premarital agreement should clearly state that there is no alimony or support in either direction.

Mandatory Paternity Tests: Some of the biggest divorce horror stories revolve around men paying child support for years only to find out it wasn't even their child. A few YouTubers asked women about their biggest fear, and the most common answer was being raped. This is a horrible and completely legitimate fear, not just in today's world but throughout history. When further pressed about how that fear made them feel, they described an extremely sickening feeling, almost as though even the thought would make them vomit. The YouTubers then told them that's the same fear and feeling men have when they wonder whether or not the child their spouse or partner had is really their child.

There are also a few statistical studies regarding paternity fraud that make their way around the Internet with the most prominent but outdated one in the Western world coming from Canada showing about 10% of men are raising a child that they believe is theirs but isn't. That study also had a figure of nearly 30%, but that was specifically related to men who suspect their spouse or partner cheated on them around the time of conception. However, more recent studies show the statistics being 17% to 33% but only when paternity was specifically being contested.

We are now living in a scientifically advanced world where paternity can quickly and easily be established through a range of different paternity tests. Society and government actually frowns upon paternity tests, and you better believe you'll get a lot of crap from every female everywhere if your ask your pregnant spouse or partner for a paternity test, especially if it is requested after she's pregnant. Here's what you'll hear:

- You think I'm a slut/she's a slut!

- Don't you trust me/her? You're just being insecure!

- I don't even see why we're/you're married if you can't trust your wife enough to not cheat!

It's all emotional garbage, and you shouldn't put up with it. If it were up to me, paternity tests would be mandatory for every birth, but the government is soundly against it. In fact, paternity tests are currently illegal in France unless the mother requests one. Why? Because 17% to 33% of the supposed fathers aren't actually the fathers when they want to contest paternity, they'd rightly refuse to pay child support for a child that isn't theirs if they knew, and now the government might be forced to step in and provide those limited resources to the mother who cheated if she can't pay for the child herself.

Child support for your child in the event of a divorce is going to be mandatory, and it is up to a court to determine which parent pays the other depending on custody and earnings. There is no getting out of it. In fact, there is currently an instance where a female high school teacher seduced her underage male student, got caught, and was allowed to resign and disappear from the community. Years later, the now adult student finds out he impregnated his teacher, she applied for public benefits for the child, and now this now 22-year-old who was raped by his teacher is being forced to provide child support payments to her. Yes, there is no getting out of it.

However, you can insist on a clause in a premarital agreement that paternity tests will be mandatory in all cases no matter what. This stops the issue from becoming a problem down the road once the spouse or partner does get pregnant.

Raising of Children: This section of the premarital agreement is the opportunity for you and your soon-to-be spouse lay out specific terms regarding the raising of children ahead of time depending on what is important to you both. Topics such as religion, schooling, holidays celebrated, and family members access and visitation are just some of the important topics to discuss. Here are some specific items or disputes I have come across during my legal career:

- He liked hunting with rifles, but she hated guns and even the thought of hunting. However, she tolerated it in her husband as long as he didn't discuss hunting other than when he was leaving to go hunting and when he would be back. When their son got old enough, he wanted to teach his son to shoot and hunt, and she was adamantly opposed to it;

- Both husband and wife were historically of the same religion, but they were only occasional attendees of church, and he only went begrudgingly. When their child was born, the wife really wanted to get back into the religion and immerse their child in it immediately with a baptism, and husband didn't want that at all; and

- Husband went to public school and believed it gave him a broader perspective on different people, financial backgrounds, and cultures that was critical later in life to his business. Wife went to a private religious school that was practically dominated by affluent white people. She wanted their child to go to the same school, while husband was completely opposed to the school (not to mention the exorbitant cost).

All of these kinds of issues can and should be worked out ahead of time with a big focus on the items that are important to each of you. You may find there are a lot of topics you care about but they don't, and they may have subjects they are adamant about, but you don't care. But all of these topics that are important one way or the other can be spelled out in the premarital agreement.

Child Support: As mentioned earlier in the book, there is going to be no way to simply reject both parties from paying child support. Different states have different rules, but many U.S. States have specific formulas written into the law that become the presumed way to calculate child support. These same laws often have specific provisions that allow for child support to be greater than what is in the formulas if there are greater needs, and some to provide less support in specific circumstances. However, how easy or difficult it is to deviate from those guidelines is also dependent on state law, and sometimes even judge to judge or court district to court district.

Because these provisions are so state-specific, you should discuss this in detail with your attorney when setting up the premarital agreement. However, as much as possible under that state law, you and your soon-to-be spouse should be waiving deviations from the guidelines and waive whatever rights you have to seek such additional support. If that is not possible, then perhaps you and your attorney can review these potential circumstances for greater support and anticipate some acceptable ways to handle financing such needs ahead of time, and those can be drafted either into this section or another one depending on your attorney's advice.

**Child Custody and Visitation**: While there are only a limited number of protections you can put in place regarding child support you may have to pay in the event of divorce, there are multiple ways to customize how custody and visitation would work. The premarital agreement, if at least fairly recent, can have the same effect as if a separate custody agreement were agreed to by both spouses in mediation and submitted to the court. Even if your spouse contests this, it is a solid starting point for developing a more updated custody agreement.

Here are the main provisions in the custody and visitation sections of a premarital agreement you need to be aware of:

- Legal versus Physical Custody. Some states have variations on the "types" of custody, but in North Carolina there is legal custody and physical custody. Legal custody refers to the ability of a parent to make major decisions regarding the child. For example, where does the child go to school, how are medical emergencies handled, and will the child be allowed to travel out of state or the country. In shared legal custody, these decisions are determined by both parents. Physical custody refers to what most people understand generally as "custody," meaning who does the child live with. In both cases, it is important to spell out what you want in the premarital agreement, and most people want equal, shared physical and legal custody.

- <u>Custody Schedule</u>. Statistically, most fathers want equal shared custody, and many mothers want full custody, but, depending on the age of the child or children, they are often better off spending equal time with each of their parents. Of course, specific situations are different for different couples, and the reasons for wanting these different versions of physical custody can vary. However, it is important to note that when one parent has more custody than the other parent, that usually comes with more child support. Take from that what you will, but as an estate planning attorney I have seen too many instances when there are deceased parents and minor children involved, there are family members who will scramble for guardianship of the children because they want to also get ahold of the money. If the money is not going to come under their control, suddenly interest in getting guardianship wanes. It is what it is.

When putting together a premarital agreement, there is usually no immediacy for child custody since there are usually no children already here. It's far easier to get agreement on equal shared custody at this point. But what exactly does that look like?

- <u>Alternate Weeks</u>. Friends of mine with one child got divorced, dad moved in with the new girlfriend (who he eventually married), but their houses were only several streets away. It became easy to set up rooms for the child in both houses, have one week at mom's house, and then have the next week at dad's house. That worked for them, but that also worked with their general work schedules. If one parent had to work late, they could spend time at the other parent's house until they got home. However, work schedules may make this arrangement too complicated.

- Split Week. Other couples with different work schedules may have to look at a typical split week arrangement. One parent will have the child during the week Monday through Friday with the exception of one specific night of the week, and then the child spends that one night and the whole weekend with the other parent. Basically, one parent gets 4 nights, and the other parent gets 3. This can also be modified a little that there is an "extra night" with the other parent during the week every other week to make it 7 nights for each parent over two weeks.

- Weekday and Weekend. This arrangement works particularly well if one parent has a more traditional Monday through Friday workday at an office, but the other parent has a job with a lot of weekend work like a wedding or event caterer. The child stays with the parent with the parent with the weekday office job on the weekends, but they spend the week with the parent has a weekend-heavy work schedule.

These general physical custody arrangements are only the beginning of the customized schedules because there are also specific exceptions such as holidays.

- Holidays: While it may start to sound like things are getting to a granular level and might seem nitpicky, many attorneys have premarital agreement templates that provide specific Holiday arrangements to start with that the parties can then modify based on their specific situation. For example, weekend custody is typically overridden so that the mother gets the children on Mother's Day and the father gets the children on Father's Day. Christmas may have Christmas Eve and the early morning with one parent, 10 a.m. on for Christmas Day with the other parent, and the next year it alternates. It's only a starting place, but it's not a horrible bargaining position to be in if these default provisions were simply left in the agreement and the marriage does fall apart.

Now there is already a Holiday schedule both parties agreed to.

- <u>Sole Custody with Visitation</u>. Life sucks sometimes, and work may have you and your spouse in residences a big distance apart. In these cases, it just makes sense for the children to be primarily with one parent most of the time with holiday weeks and even the entire school summer with the other parent. There may also be periodic visits when the children go to the other parent, or the parent goes to the children's hometown for a visit. (It is important to note that this is almost never a choice in a premarital agreement, but it is an option you should be aware of.)

As you can see, custody and visitation can be complex and have many options. While this is a premarital agreement and it is likely that there are no children from the relationship yet, getting these terms locked in as being as equal as possible now means it becomes more of an uphill battle for a spouse to seek something different in the event of a divorce.

Estate Terms: There are extremely standard clauses in premarital agreements designed to allow both spouses to plan their own estates however they want without interference from the other, and while having the spouse waive any statutory rights, they may have to get an "elective share" of your estate. While the language is often short and clear, it can become extremely important if you pass on while the children are still young, you want to leave most or all of your estate to your children… but you want one of your friends or relatives to be in charge of the money rather than your spouse. Don't let your attorney overlook this particular section.

Maintenance of A Premarital Agreement

There are a few simpler but critical steps to take in making sure your premarital agreement is maintained. Situations and assets may change, so it's important to periodically reflect those changes.

- **"Refresh" the Premarital Agreement every few years**. Having an otherwise valid prenup thrown out because it was "stale" amounts to laziness and lack of persistence. At a maximum, a premarital agreement should be reviewed, reworked, and the revised contract executed every five years. It's also not crazy to handle this process every three years. The asset lists of separate and joint property should be updated, but this is also an opportunity to reaffirm the core elements of the prenup.

- **Ensure the Updated Prenup is Reviewed by Both Attorneys**. It's not enough for you to just go through an updated agreement, print it out, and ask your spouse to sign it. They can always claim that they never read it, or they can claim that they didn't understand the terms since it had been 3-5 years since they last looked at it. By making sure your spouse's attorney reviewed the agreement and met with your spouse to discuss it, there is no way for them to feign ignorance about what was in the document as a way to get a judge to throw it out.

- **<u>Be Ready to Walk Away</u>**. If it was a struggle to get your spouse to sign the premarital agreement in the first place, then it might be even more difficult getting them to sign an updated version every few years. However, you should never simply accept the fact that your spouse won't sign it again and just continue in the marriage. You should always be ready to walk away from the marriage, especially if they are refusing to update and sign a revised agreement. Basically, if you are already married with a prenup and they are refusing to renew it, there is a very good chance they would rather have your money than you. This is the time to walk away, because the longer you wait to leave, the greater risk of the premarital agreement will be set aside in the divorce.

Having a premarital agreement is just one of the components in a divorce protection system, but it is a critical component. However, the agreement has to be done correctly by a professional who knows what they are doing, under the right circumstances to hold up in court, and it needs to be revised and renewed every few years. Without this agreement being as rock solid as possible, the other components may fall by the wayside as well.

Chapter Eight:
Corporate Entities, Contracts, and Specific Assets

"OK, what am I signing this time?" Rick asked.

Rick Paulson, his cousin Rob Paulson, and Rob's attorney Chuck Ocean sat around a different conference room table at Chuck's bigger office. They were all moving up in the world.

"It's to form a new Wyoming LLC so we can purchase the new property Rob wants," Chuck answered.

It always sounded more complicated than it seemed until Chuck explained it, typically with a note pad, pen, and drawings of boxes within boxes. This layering of assets inside corporate entities, and corporate entities within the trust seemed complex, but it really wasn't.

"We're buying that house we looked at last week," Rob replied while Chuck started drawing. "Since we're renting this one out, it should be protected inside some corporate entity, and accountant said a limited liability company would be the best way to do it."

"Exactly," Chuck said pointing at the box within a larger box. "This is the LLC we're forming now, and you are the sole member of the LLC representing the trust as the real owner."

"That's right," Rick said leaning closer and nodding his head. "Just like the last rental real estate purchase a few years back that Cassie and I are still renting. Remind me again, why Wyoming? Why not our state?"

"Because having Wyoming corporate entities inside a Wyoming Domestic Asset Protection Trust ties us to Wyoming's jurisdiction and protective laws a little more firmly," Chuck replied.

"If I'm remembering the research I did via Google University the first time we did a purchase like this, there were fees for both states, though, since we're basically running a Wyoming business here," Rick said. "Is it worth the extra fees to get this complicated?"

"I cringe every time I see the accountant's report showing those expenses coming out of the trust," Rob interjected before Chuck could answer. "But it's better than losing a hundred percent in a lawsuit or fifty percent in a divorce."

"Amen to that," Rick said, nodding his head.

Just owning assets titled in your separate name doesn't protect you from losing them in divorce, and it certainly doesn't insulate you from lawsuits. And one of the worst things you could do is own business assets in your own name as a sole proprietor. By personally owning assets like rental property, you not only subject the property from lawsuits by tenants, their guests, and other parties, but you also open up all of your other assets to collection from judgments. So how can you protect yourself from business lawsuits while simultaneously reinforcing the Divorce Firewall?

Treat your assets engaged in business as actual businesses with all of the corporate formalities required and have your Domestic Asset Protection Trust own those business interests. The plan is that simple, but, as you'll see, it takes ongoing work and maintenance to make this protection a reality. Let's start with an overview of the main corporate entities (ignoring those that don't provide protection); go over typical assets owned in these entities; and then move into how these businesses should be owned, controlled, and integrated with the Divorce Firewall strategy.

Entities Overview

Limited Liability Companies

Limited Liability Companies, frequently shortened to "LLCs," were originally designed to provide corporate protection to partnerships. If two or more people wanted to go into business but not have the formalities of setting up a corporation, issuing stock, and keeping specific meetings and minutes throughout the year, they could create a partnership but had to give up corporate protection. State legislatures saw this as being unfair, and so they created limited liability companies for businesses to function like a partnership but also have the all-important benefits of insulating the partners, called "members" in LLCs, from personal liability from business activities. The typical process is filing "Articles of Organization" with the proper state agency, create an Operating Agreement that describes how the LLC is run, and the members have "Membership Interests" in relation to their ownership percentages. When it comes to the actual management of the LLC, either the members can run everything just like a traditional partnership, but there can also be one or more Managers to do the actual day to day running of business.

Over time, as limited liability companies grew in popularity, the laws and regulations around LLCs dropped the requirement for needing two or more members and allowed individuals to also create these easier-to-manage business entities. Depending on the state, there could also be extremely limited lawsuit remedies available against the LLCs. For example, in North Carolina when an LLC has a judgment against it or one of the members has a personal judgment against them, then the only remedy is a "charging order," which means that LLC profits or the member's share of the profits is the only way for the judgment to get paid. The person with the judgment can only garnish the profits. However, the LLC can take a variety of actions to make sure there are no profits distributed by increasing salaries, making asset purchases, or other methods.

On the tax side, there are some deductions and credits available to LLCs that aren't available or the same as corporations, and there are some deductions and credits available to corporations that aren't available to LLCs. In addition, it is possible for a single member LLC to be taxed as an S-Corporation, which has its own set of rules. Before choosing any corporate entity for a particular business, be sure to find a good accountant to advise you on the tax ramifications of the different entities so you can make the right choice.

Corporations

The long-standing, traditional entity for protecting personal assets from business lawsuits is the corporation. One or more people get together to create a business, they generate and submit the proper paperwork often called Articles of Incorporation with a state to form the corporation, and then issue stock to the founders as agreed upon. The corporation creates Bylaws that describes how the corporation is run, and there typically needs to be a Board of Directors as well as corporate officers.

These formalities need to be handled the right way, and, unlike an LLC, the corporation must hold regular meetings of the board of directors and the shareholders. By law, these meetings are often required at least annually, and meeting minutes need to be written and kept with the company's corporate records. The corporation typically

Limited Partnerships

Limited Partnerships used in business can insulate the passive investors, called limited partners, from personal liability while putting one or more general partners on the hook for all of the actions of the company. While at first this sounds like a terrible way to do business if you are the general partner since you are exposing yourself to personal liability, you don't need to directly own those general partnership interests. Instead, the general partnership interests can be owned by a limited liability company or corporation in which you have control (directly as the owner or indirectly as a corporate officer or manager). In many cases, several businesses already held through corporations or limited liability companies are layered inside a family limited partnership.

Why arrange a business this way? The usual reasons for setting up one or more small businesses under the umbrella of a so-called family limited partnership. While there is no such actual entity called a family limited partnership, the "family" label is attached in many situations since one or more family members are usually involved in the business, and the intention is to eventually pass the entity down to the next generation. However, the current generation typically wants to maintain complete control over everything while transferring value during their lifetime in the form of gifts. The general partnership interests typically comprise only one percent (1%) for each general partner, and the rest of the limited shares bring the total percentage up to one hundred percent (100%).

During life, the current generation will gift limited partnership interests to the next generation since it conveys value in the company reducing the taxable estate without actually giving away any control in the business operations. We'll explore an example of this later using Rob Paulson and his family as an example.

S-Corporations

S-Corporations are not actual legal entities since "S-Corporation Status" refers simply to a method of small businesses being taxed by the government. Basically, small businesses are given a tax break by not being taxed at the company level and then again at the personal level. This special status is available for smaller corporations and even limited liability companies in some situations. If a corporation does not elect to be taxed as an S-Corporation, then it by default is a C-Corporation. Here are the two basic examples:

- After divorcing Karen, Bill Peterson finally gets his head on right, starts a new business, and he makes a lot of profit as a C-Corporation since he never got around to filing the S-Corporation election. If the company makes $500,000 profit but Bill paid himself a $200,000 salary, a rough estimate of Bill's overall taxes is $264,871, leaving Bill about $235,129 to pay Karen's alimony and child support.

- If Rob Paulson had a similar business but took the time to file the S-Corporation election and put himself on a $200,000 salary as Bill did, his taxes would be calculated just as if all of the income were his rather than being taxed at the corporate level first, and his tax bill would be $187,921 leaving him $312,079, giving Rob $76,950 more because he filed as an S-Corporation.

Please note that the S-Corporation election is a simple federal form to file for businesses, but it is very likely this status is not available with some of the additional corporate and trust protection strategies being used here. Consult a tax professional to see what is the best tax option for you and weigh that against the protections outlined in this book. (Some people would be happy paying more in taxes if it meant they weren't risking losing half of their assets in a divorce).

For more information, go to www.DivorceFirewall.com

State and Jurisdiction of Entity

While technically the corporate entities can be formed under the laws of the state that makes the most sense for business operations and corporate protection, it is also highly recommended you look to the state you are forming the Domestic Asset Protection Trust under. For example, if you are looking at Wyoming as one of the states that would make sense to form your trust, then having the corporate entities also formed under Wyoming law makes a lot of divorce protection sense. Now not only are the minimal assets needed to make your Domestic Asset Protection Trust qualify under Wyoming law, you are also bringing in all of the business interests to Wyoming, fortifying against any potential argument that the trust is only falling under Wyoming law as a formality.

Of course, this facet of bringing your businesses under Wyoming law needs to be balanced against any variance taxes, additional state fees, and corporate paperwork and filings for your business to be based in another state as a "foreign" corporate entity being authorized to do business in that state. Yes, it can be complicated, but that is why having a good accountant and other professionals to review the pros and cons is critical. In all, everything has to be balanced against the potential jeopardy of losing half in a divorce, so the complications may be well worth the additional work if a divorce disaster strikes.

Assets in Business

Now that we have examined some of the basic corporate structures, let's take a look at some of the typical assets that deserve both corporate and divorce protection that can be held inside a corporate entity.

Real estate

One of the most valuable growth assets a person can own is real estate. While stocks can certainly grow over the long haul, residential and commercial real estate is not going to disappear if the stock market collapses. Whether it is the house you live in, use as a vacation property, or lease out, you can make the property business property if you choose to. Yes, this definitely makes things more complicated, but it could be a valuable addition to your Divorce Firewall strategy if you are willing to put up with the complex details and have a good accountant.

But how do you turn personal real estate into business property? It has to be an asset used in business. If you have vacation property you like to use several times a year, why not rent it out the rest or even part of the year? This means having a management company handle the rentals, repairs, and clean up between guests, unless this is something you want to handle yourself.

Growing up in Rhode Island, the beaches of Narragansett were a bustling and energetic place to be from Memorial Day to Labor Day, and the area flooded with tourists and vacationers renting houses on a weekly basis. However, the area became much more calm and serene during the off-season. Many people owned homes within walking distance of a beach as a business investment, never occupying the homes themselves. From late May through early September, they collected a ton of cash for weekly rentals, and they were usually solidly booked throughout the season. But what about the off-season? The University of Rhode Island wasn't that far away, and they ended up renting the houses at a fraction of the summer rates for the school year. On the other hand, my grandparents owned a house within two blocks of the beach and only rented out the house during the school year so we could have the family use the house all Summer. It all depends on what you want to do, but by even having the house in a corporation or limited liability company with several weeks or months being rented out, you can legitimately have the company owned by Domestic Asset Protection Trust rather than own the house directly, and you now have another layer that a divorce (or other lawsuit) has to get through to lay claim to your assets.

But what about your personal residence? Surely that can't be considered a business asset. It can. If your trustee uses the same process to purchase the house you want to live in through a limited liability company or corporation owned by the Domestic Asset Protection Trust, then the company can lease the house to you and your spouse. And now you can both pay rent in accordance with the terms of the premarital agreement. So not only are you taking your primary residence off the table for divorce, but you are also channeling the percentage of the rent your spouse is obligated to pay into your Domestic Asset Protection Trust via the company. (See later in the book how the lease for your own residence should read in order to get you the best divorce protection possible.)

When discussing this idea, I often hear "That sounds great in theory, but how can you convince your spouse to go along with this arrangement?" The best argument for it is by encouraging your spouse/future spouse to have their own real estate which can be rented out. Now they are building equity in their own house, the tenants are at least paying for any mortgage and other expenses of the house, and your spouse may even have some profits left over.

Automobiles

If you don't own a vehicle, then you can't lose it in a divorce. That's just one factor in the whole "lease versus own" debate over vehicles, even though it usually isn't one of the first factors most people consider, if they consider it all. But what if you could both save money by buying the vehicle but then not own it for purposes of divorce?

The simplest strategy to do this is to set up a limited liability company through the Domestic Asset Protection Trust, have the trust put money into an account in the company's name, and then make the cash purchase of the car in the name of the company. The LLC can now lease the car to you as an individual. Now not only are you insulated from the car being on the table for a divorce if a judge tries to get around the premarital agreement, but you leasing the car from the LLC funnels your own money into your trust so that can't be on the table for a divorce any more than if you leased the car from an outside company.

Want to take this a step further? What if your spouse wants a new car, your trust can afford to buy the car they want, and then it can be leased back to you. You can then work with the trustee of the Domestic Asset Protection Trust to arrange for the purchase through a company owned by the trust. Then you can provide the leased car, or even have your spouse pay part or all of the lease rather than the money going to some other company. In the event of a divorce, you aren't going to lose the car since it isn't yours… but you can transfer the lease over to your spouse if they want to keep up the payments. (For this last part of the strategy, it is critical to reference any such leases in the premarital agreement or an update to it, and how such lease would be treated in the event of a divorce.)

Other Businesses

There are many different kinds of business opportunities, and just about all of them should be viewed for inclusion in your Domestic Asset Protection Trust. If you decided to invest in some franchise fast food locations, then they could be owned through one or more corporate entities and the entities could be owned by the trust. How about a 24-hour gym? Again, there is no reason it can't be purchased through a corporate entity owned by your protective trust. Hair salons and spas? Convenience stores? The only potential impediment to any of these businesses being owned through a corporate entity which is in turn owned by the Domestic Asset Protection Trust would be prohibitions through any franchise agreements and not the law.

What if this isn't passive investments but you are engaged in an active business that is providing you your regular salary and income? That still doesn't mean that it can't go into the Domestic Asset Protection Trust. For instance, in Rob Paulson's case he has his own firm as a financial advisor through a limited liability company, and his Domestic Asset Protection Trust owns the LLC. As you'll see in the next section, while ownership of the corporation or LLC is titled in the name of the Domestic Asset Protection Trust, the actual operations can still be in your control.

How the entities are run and how the trust owns them

Ownership of any business entities you are using in the Divorce Firewall Strategy should be titled in the name of trust. But what exactly does this mean for the different entities, and how can you maintain some measure of control over your own businesses? It's really not complicated when you can separate ownership from control. We'll review all of the corporate entities and how they are typically done. (We are ignoring the S-Corporation since it is really a tax classification). However, for more information on how control versus ownership of entities is handled state to state, check with an accountant and attorney licensed in the state you are considering.

Limited Liability Companies

Limited liability companies can have members and managers, and, depending on the state, you can elect to have just members, or both members and managers. For purposes of the Divorce Firewall Strategy and maintaining control, you want to make sure the LLC is being formed to allow both members and managers. With the Domestic Asset Protection Trust being owned by the trust, or more specifically in the name of the trustee as trustee for the trust. The trustee is the actual legal member representing the interests of the trust. But just because the trustee is the member doesn't mean that they also have to be the manager or a manager.

If this is your business being operated by you, then there is no reason you can't be the official manager in the Operating Agreement and meeting minutes of the limited liability company. This allows you to transact business on behalf of the LLC, handle banking and operational matters, and basically run the entire company. In this sense, you are only beholden to the trustee of your trust since they are the member and official "owner." In addition, depending on the state the Domestic Asset Protection Trust is formed in, you can also maintain trust-level control over business assets as the Investment Asdvisor.

Corporations

Corporations are a little more formal than limited liability companies, and there are more roles in the traditional corporation than with an LLC. But, once again, you can maintain a lot of control over the business operations. A corporation has shareholders, and the corporate shares should be owned by the trustee of the Domestic Asset Protection Trust on behalf of the trust. As an example, if John Smith is the trustee, the ownership on the actual share certificates for Rob Paulson's business XYZ Consulting, Inc. could read "John Smith, as Trustee of the Paulson Domestic Asset Protection Trust."

But who actually controls the corporation? Corporations have a board of directors who are elected by the shareholders, and the board of directors elects the corporate officers to manage the business. Depending on state law, it is entirely possible that there can be only one member of the board of directors, and the trustee can elect you as that member of the board. You can then turn around and elect yourself as president of the corporation. Once again depending on state law, you can also appoint yourself as corporate secretary and treasurer, and then as a succession and safety measure name your trustee as the vice-president to take over should anything happen to you. (Some states require that the president and corporate secretary be different people, and in that case the trustee or someone else you trust can be the corporate secretary.)

For all practical purposes, you have no direct ownership in the corporation but total control of its operations, and as with the LLC you can also have some trust-level control as the trust's Investment Advisor.

Limited Partnerships

Let me start by saying that using a limited partnership is at another level in corporate ownership and control, and it is often only being used at a more advanced level later in a business development strategy. A lot of my clients who look at limited partnerships are doing so as part of a family limited partnership strategy to start transferring wealth without control to the next generation, so this may not be how you would want to initially set up your businesses. Next, the family limited partnership (FLP for short) is usually set up with several LLCs and corporations inside the FLP rather than in the Domestic Asset Protection, and then the FLP is set up in conjunction with the trust.

With those factors in mind, if you do want to use a limited partnership as part of your overall Divorce Firewall Strategy, then here are how the ownership interests are handled (and, yes, this is complicated):

- The general partnership shares are owned by a corporation or limited liability company;

- The corporation or limited liability company owning the general partnership shares are owned by the Domestic Asset Protection Trust; and

- The limited shares are owned directly by the Domestic Asset Protection Trust.

Let's keep this part of the example simple and assume that the accountants and attorneys recommended a limited liability company own the general partnership shares. The general partnership shares comprise one percent (1%) of the total family limited partnership, leaving ninety-nine percent (99%) in limited partnership shares. Since all of the control is vested in the owner of the general partnership shares, the limited liability company completely controls the FLP. In order to keep control over the FLP without ownership, you can be the manager of the LLC and the trustee can be the member acting on behalf of the trust.

Yes, this setup is complicated and has several layers, but if you start considering transferring value to your beneficiaries without transferring control in order to reduce a potential 40% or more in estate taxes on your business, this strategy may start to make more sense down the road.

Summary

There are a variety of corporate entities and setups that can bring the Divorce Firewall Strategy to another level of not just divorce protection but also legal protection. It is more complicated and needs a good team of professionals to help make sure everything is done correctly, but if you intend to build wealth through real estate and businesses, then you need to consider these entities and strategies.

Chapter Nine:
Contracts, Leases, and Other Agreements

"I've been evicted from my own home?" Stacy asked her attorney. "How could you let this happen?"

"Whoa, wait a minute," her attorney interjected. "I warned you this could happen the last time we updated the prenup and the new lease was signed."

"No you didn't," Stacy automatically responded, realizing her attorney was right before she even finished the sentence.

"Yes I did, and I have the notes to prove it," he responded evenly. "First of all, it's not an eviction. I told you when I reviewed the lease on the house that it was a month to month arrangement, and all it would take was for the lease to not be renewed, so under the law all you get is 30 days' notice. So it's not an eviction with the usual process. You do have 30 days to find a temporary place to live, and Rob and his stuff is already out of the house."

"What about the kids?" Stacy asked sarcastically. "Are they being thrown out on the street, too?"

"Well, no," Stacy's attorney responded, a little hesitation in his voice. "I already spoke to Rob's attorney, and he told me the kids can leave all of their stuff in place."

"That doesn't make any sense," Stacy said, now genuinely confused. "If the lease isn't being renewed and I have 30 days to get out, then how can the kids not be moving out at the same time?"

"It took some back and forth, but I got an answer to that question," her attorney told her. "But I'm sure you're not going to like the answer. The house is owned by a limited liability company, and that's who you and Rob have been paying rent to. It turns out that the limited liability company is actually owned by the trust that Rob set up before you got married and which was referenced in the premarital agreement as Rob's separate property."

"What?" Stacy practically screamed into the phone. "I thought Rick owned the property since he's the one who signed the lease."

"No, Rick is the Trustee of Rob's trust," Stacy's attorney acknowledged. "He signed the lease on behalf of the company. Rob basically owns the house you've been renting through that company and his trust. Rob's attorney has told me a new lease has already been signed for the rental of the house to Rob alone, so he will be moving back into the house once you have moved out. But your children's furniture and possessions don't have to be moved at all since Rob is OK with them keeping their current rooms for when they stay with him. That will actually cause them a little less disruption when…"

Stacy hung up the phone on her attorney and wept.

In the past few chapters, we have discussed some of the most important contracts and agreements in the Divorce Firewall Strategy, but there are some others to keep in mind and consider. This chapter will definitely be shorter than the others, but that doesn't make the correct use of these agreements any less important if needed.

We'll start with an agreement used at some point early in the dating process, move to a lease agreement vital to keeping real estate insulated, and finish up with one clever way to fend off the possibility of even emergency alimony if you have a business.

**Acknowledgement of Non-Residence**: Early in the dating phase, there may be sexual encounters, but spending the night at one another's places may be a whole other ballgame. It can become easy for a couple to naturally "fall into" staying over at each other's places, but this could become a disaster at a moment's notice. This is especially true if the person you are with reveals themselves to be a bit unstable.

I know you have heard the stories before, and it definitely impacts men more than women. A woman has stayed over a few nights, and now there is an argument. A switch is flipped, and suddenly she's smashing breakables, throwing heavy objects at you, and refuses to leave. The police are called... and she claims you attacked her, and that she lives there.

I'm sure there are other books, video channels, and other content to provide advice on when to turn on your phone's video recorder so you can show the police. In today's world, particularly in the U.S., even that might not be enough to save you from going to jail that night. But even if it was enough proof to keep the handcuffs off of you, who do you think is going to be forced to leave the house and who gets to stay?

That is unless you have a signed acknowledgement from her that she is a guest at your residence and doesn't live there.

This can be a simple document that can list both of your names, the address of your residence, them acknowledging that they don't live there, and that you would only ever cohabitate with an executed Cohabitation Agreement. Of course, this is also something you should gladly be willing to sign for their residence acknowledging that you are nothing more than a guest at the same time.

"

That conversation must be awkward," you might be thinking. How should you approach even getting a conversation like that going. If there is even a hint at them wanting to spend the night at your place, you need to stop whatever you were doing and ask them to sit down because you need to talk to them about something serious. Then you tell them that you very much would like for them to spend the night from time to time, but you (or someone you know) had a horrible experience when the person they were dating flipped out, started breaking things, and then the police showed up only to kick them out of their own house.

The next day when they were allowed back into their own place, it was destroyed. You (or the person you know) were so traumatized at just how much was lost, and there was absolutely nothing they could do without a bunch of expensive lawyers. However, you/they were then told about an Acknowledgement of Non-Residence form that simply stated the person whose name was filled in was only a guest at their place and did not live there. You would not only like for them to sign one before staying over because it would give you peace of mind, but you also want to make sure that they have peace of mind when you sign one for their place.

You may initially get a lot of grief, but hopefully the next day there will be more cooperation and they'll agree to sign. If not, then either move on or only agree to sleepovers at their place so you can be the one to leave when you want.

Real Estate Leases (For You)

Some potential techniques within the Divorce Firewall Strategy include leasing your own property to yourself through a corporation or limited liability company which is owned by your Domestic Asset Protection Trust. First, it should go without saying but in order to solidly protect your real estate from not only being on the table for a divorce but also keeping it away from lawsuits, bankruptcy, creditors, and disability benefits loss, all of the formalities have to be observed. As an attorney the number of times I have been told that there was a contract, lease, or agreement when there was actually never anything in writing is staggering. It falls in line with the same people who believe they are properly setting up a protective corporation for their business by filing Articles of Incorporation but then never creating bylaws, not assigning board members and officers, and neglecting to hold annual meetings and create written meeting minutes. So, yes, there has to be an actual lease in writing.

The next critical component is to charge reasonable rent under the lease agreement. If the rent is only a token amount and not in line with comparable properties in the area, then there is every possibility a judge could see through the corporate layer of the protection you are trying to achieve. It may take a lot more to get through to the other assets in the Domestic Asset Protection Trust, but why chance it?

Finally, the duration of the lease needs to line up with your goals, and not a spouse or anyone else. If leasing your own property through the corporate structure and Domestic Asset Protection Trust is only for you, then there is no reason not to make it an annual lease. On the other hand, if this is a lease between you and a spouse and they are to be paying you as part of the premarital agreement, then having a quicker way out may make sense. Therefore, the lease may only be month-to-month.

Employment Contract for a Spouse

This last one is really for those who are already married, have a spouse that doesn't have their own career, but they are helping out one or more of your businesses. This is not an ideal situation, but if you find yourself in this situation, then you might as well protect yourself from any possibility of emergency alimony by engaging your spouse through an employment contract. (Of course, the preferred option is to make sure your spouse has their own career outside your business).

Depending on your type of business and where it is located, giving your spouse an actual job with an employment contract can come with some tax benefits, provide a source of income for your spouse while simultaneously getting work out of them, and ensure that emergency alimony is not something that is on the table.

However, there are some pretty stringent guidelines to keep in mind if you find yourself in this situation:

- Always have an impartial direct supervisor over your spouse, and remain hands off. This way if there is a separation or divorce, you can't be accused of trying to push her out and have that emergency alimony claim kick in.

- Have a legitimate need for their services. If there is not an actual need to have an employee in your business, then you are just throwing money away. It's no different just because the employee is your spouse.

- If there is a divorce or separation, be prepared to keep them on as long as they are performing well, but be prepared to document shortcomings and warnings leading up to a firing. While it is not likely that a spouse would want to continue working in your business after divorce, you have to let them quit or legitimately mess up so badly that they should be fired. And you should never be the one doing the firing. Leave that to their direct supervisor.

- If they do want to leave, have their supervisor provide as glowing a job recommendation as warranted to help them find that job.

Again, this is not the ideal situation, but it is a technique to keep in mind if the situation comes up.

Chapter Ten:
Trusts and Other Legacy Planning Documents

"We've been married for twelve years now and have three children together," Rob Paulson said to his attorney. *"I want to leave her something in the estate plan despite what we have in the premarital agreement, but I want to do it the right way. At the same time, I want to start making sure the main inheritance for the children is set up the right way."*

"That's all understandable," Rob's attorney Chuck Ocean said. *"I wouldn't suggest doing anything major with the Domestic Asset Protection Trust, like changing it around. And to do that, we would basically have to create a new trust and then move all of the assets to the new trust with the new provisions. We do have an easier way to handle it."*

Once again, Chuck pulled out his notepad to start drawing his boxes.

"Do you want to give your children even better asset protection than you have with your own trust for the rest of their lives?" Chuck asked.

"Of course," Rob said, leaning a little closer to the table so he could see the notepad better.

"Good," the attorney replied. *"What we can do is set up Asset Management Trusts for each of the children. Instead of their inheritance ever going directly to them, it will be held in their trust for their benefit with a different trustee."*

"Like Rick is the trustee for my trust, right?" Rob asked.

"Exactly," Chuck said. "The inheritance you provide them can be directed out of your trust and into these Asset Management Trusts through a back door we set up in your Domestic Asset Protection Trust. All we have to do is change your Will. We can also have the relatively smaller inheritance coming out of your revocable living trust and other sources directly go to the kids' trusts."

"What about Stacy?" Rob asked. "I did want to do something for her as well."

"This is the best part because it's flexible," Chuck said. "As long as we're already changing your revocable living trust to reflect the new trusts for the kids, we can take out a big life insurance policy on you, make the revocable trust the beneficiary, and list in the revocable trust that the insurance money goes to Stacy."

"How is that flexible?" Rob questioned.

"Because we can direct the life insurance to go to Stacy under certain circumstances," Chuck continued. "She only gets the money if she's still married to you and not separated with the intention of divorce. So if anything like that happens, then the life insurance money just goes to the kids' trusts with everything else."

There were a lot of boxes and arrows on the notepad now, but it was making sense. Best of all, he was able to provide something for the wife he loved without making a major change to his plan… as long as she didn't do anything to cause a divorce.

The Domestic Asset Protection Trust is just one trust in the Divorce Firewall System, there are other "estate planning" documents you will need, and there are also a few other trusts you should consider both before marriage and as life progresses. I have conveniently put them in the sections Basic, Advanced, or Spousal to benefit the spouse. The Basic section contains the documents you absolutely should have as part of your Divorce Firewall System if you are serious enough to enact a Domestic Asset Protection

Trust. The Advanced section reviews documents that are recommended if you have children and wish to provide for them after you pass on in a more protected manner than most people do. And finally, there may be instances you want to provide for a spouse but not disrupt anything in your strategy, especially the Domestic Asset Protection Trust.

Basic Estate Planning Documents

Revocable Living Trust: Often discussed as the great alternative to using a Will to distribute your property after death, a Revocable Living Trust also distributes the trust property the way you wish after death but does so without having the trust assets go through the probate court process first. It also provides effective management of assets for underage beneficiaries, can protect inheritances for special needs beneficiaries, and plan effectively for many different contingencies. It can also effectively put in place safeguards to manage your trust assets during a time when you are incapacitated without having to get a legal guardian appointed to you by the court.

This trust will efficiently handle assets you are keeping outside of the Domestic Asset Protection Trust should you become incapacitated or pass on without a court being involved, so while it may not contain the bulk of your assets, it should contain the bulk of your non-retirement assets not protected by the DAPT.

Financial Power of Attorney: While the revocable living trust handles trust assets (outside of the DAPT) during a period when you are incapacitated, there are often tax reasons not to put all of your assets immediately into a revocable living trust. This is where the Financial Power of Attorney comes in. This document empowers your appointed "agent" to handle financial transactions for accounts outside the trust as well as dealing with government agencies, applying for benefits, and even signing tax returns. Of course, if using a Will-based plan, the Financial Power of Attorney would handle all of your financial accounts if you were incapacitated but not deceased.

__Health Care Power of Attorney__: While a Revocable Living Trust in combination with a Financial Power of Attorney can handle your assets, the people you choose to handle finances may not be the same people you would want to make health care decisions for you. After all, the two functions require different skill sets, attitudes, and knowledge. This may be especially true for a spouse having control over finances but whom you may be perfectly fine with handling health and medical decisions for you.

For couples, they generally want each other to make health decisions first and then will each list a succession of individuals who are in charge in the event of a medical crisis rather than relying on the state statutes to determine what person or group of people are in charge of your medical decisions. Very few of our clients want ALL of their children or ALL of their siblings trying to agree on every medical decision that needs to be made.

__Living Will__: A Living Will is also called a "Declaration of a Desire for a Natural Death" or "Advanced Directive" in some states or jurisdictions. This is often a very specific document related to the end-of-life decision of whether or not to withhold life support and artificial nutrition and hydration if there is no hope of recovery, and some states provide a variety of other major care decisions.

For example, in North Carolina where I am a licensed attorney, the specific conditions we draft into a Living Will is that two attending physicians (doctors who have actually examined you) agree that you are either in a persistent vegetative state or are terminal and incurable before taking action. In non-medical terms, the doctors don't believe there is anything they can do for you and keeping you on life support and nutrition/hydration is only prolonging the inevitable. At that point, your choices kick in. The main benefits of having this document are 1) that your wishes in this matter are given legal effect, and 2) no one has to actually give the order to withhold treatment because you have already done so in writing.

Nomination of Conservator: In terms of health care, the Health Care Power of Attorney and Living Will should be all that is needed in an extreme medical crisis. The Financial Power of Attorney and Trusts should be all that is needed to take care of your finances in an extreme medical crisis. But sometimes there are relatives or friends who think they know better than the people you have appointed to make these decisions, and so they try to get "guardianship" or "conservatorship" over you.

Getting guardianship over you could be a backdoor way for someone, even a spouse, to try to get control over your finances. However, being clear in a Nomination of Conservator about who you want to make financial decisions for you puts up a substantial roadblock to that, especially if the same list of people line up with your trustee and financial power of attorney agent lists.

Pour-Over Will: This is a specific Last Will and Testament used as a safety valve to send any assets that inadvertently end up in probate over to the revocable living trust to be distributed. In some cases, like tax refunds or rebates, there is no option for the government or company to make the check payable to your trust, and so probate becomes necessary for those assets. This Will names executors and may have a few specific provisions, but by and large it simply names your trust as the beneficiary of the estate for what limited assets end up in probate.

Advanced Documents

There are also some specific trusts that could come into play when you are setting up your Divorce Firewall System or added later as circumstances change. The biggest changed circumstance would be having children, and a close second could be wanting (or negotiating in a prenup update) to provide an estate for your spouse. These items can always be added later and integrated into the rest of your plans with some updates.

When it comes to children, receiving and inheritance outright from you can put them in the same vulnerable position you were trying to avoid by having a Domestic Asset Protection Trust in the first place. The only difference is you can protect the wealth you would be leaving your child with fewer formalities and requirements than you had to protect the money you earned through your DAPT. Here are the two main protective trusts we use:

Asset Management Trusts: An Asset Management Trust is an extremely powerful tool for preserving an estate beyond the first level beneficiaries, who are often the children. Instead of the Revocable Living Trust or Domestic Asset Protection Trust distributing assets directly to the children it would instead move assets into each child's separate Asset Management Trust. Each Asset Management Trust now operates with a trustee other than the beneficiary completely in charge. If the beneficiary gets embroiled in a lawsuit, goes through a divorce, or becomes disabled and receives disability benefits/Medicaid, then the trustee has absolute discretion whether or not to distribute assets, much like the DAPT, and therefore these trust assets remain protected throughout the child's lifetime. In addition, the assets in the Asset Management Trust can now pass estate tax free to the beneficiary's children (often your grandchildren) provided the correct tax forms were taken care of by an accountant upon your death to apply "generation skipping tax exemptions." (No, you don't want me to go there in this book because this is all complicated enough). With estate tax rates currently as high as 40%, this can be a tremendous savings for the second-generation beneficiaries while simultaneously protecting the children during their lifetimes.

**IRA Trusts**: While estate taxes can be a huge consideration in planning, people often neglect to look at income taxes on retirement accounts for an inheritance. One of the best ways to avoid a huge income tax inheritance hit AND get ten years to spread out income taxes in the next generation is through an IRA Trust for each child and having the IRA Trusts named as the beneficiary of your retirement accounts rather than naming the beneficiary directly. (The accounts paying into the IRA Trust don't have to be just IRAs, but it can include any tax-deferred account like 401ks, 403bs, and even Roth accounts). This trust also provides the same lawsuit, divorcing spouse, and disability/Medicaid protection of the Asset Management Trust. In addition, the IRA Trust can be integrated with the Asset Management Trust so that after the ten years of maximizing income tax savings the IRA Trusts can simply transfer the assets into the beneficiary's corresponding Asset Management Trust.

Spousal Support Documents

The Divorce Firewall Strategy is about planning ahead of a marriage to make sure that a divorce won't destroy your own finances. After all, there is a 50% or so divorce rate out there. But that also means that there are also successful marriages where spouses may want to provide for the other. In addition, as the years go on and the premarital agreement is revised over time, there may be some negotiating going on regarding estate wishes. This doesn't have to be accomplished by undoing any of the protective steps you have taken so far, and it doesn't mean abandoning the Domestic Asset Protection Trust naming your children (or their Asset Management Trusts) as beneficiary, but it could mean adding a few elements:

Life Insurance with Revocable Living Trust (Advanced):
Providing for your spouse if they survive you can be as simple as buying and maintaining a life insurance policy. However, rather than simply providing a payout directly to your spouse, it's possible to provide benefits to your spouse in a protected way through the revocable living trust you are setting up anyway. Now, there is no one way this must be done, and a lot may depend on whether this is done through the goodness of your heart or as a negotiated point when refreshing a premarital agreement during the course of the marriage. Here are some possibilities:

- The life insurance can pay into the revocable living trust, and the revocable living trust simply states that if your spouse outlives you, that the life insurance pays to the spouse. If your spouse dies before you, then the life insurance is directed to be paid to your other beneficiaries, likely your children, along with everything else;

- The life insurance proceeds are to be used by the Trustee to buy an immediate annuity to provide lifetime income to the spouse;

- The life insurance payout is to be held in trust to be used for the spouse in sole discretion of the Trustee, so they have a safety cushion, but the money is not controlled by the spouse nor given to them outright; and

- The life insurance death benefit is to be held in trust and used in sole discretion of the Trustee as above, but there can be a different list of trustees and successor trustees just overseeing the life insurance who are more acceptable to the spouse, such as one of the kids, their siblings, or the spouse's other family members.

The premarital agreement should mention whether or not the insurance is to be maintained after a divorce or not, if the beneficiary can be changed after a divorce or not, and if the policy is to be transferred to the spouse after a divorce so the future premiums are their responsibility.

Spousal IRA Trust: Another way to provide for a spouse using assets outside of the Domestic Asset Protection Trust could be letting the spouse inherit one or more retirement accounts. However, rather than simply naming the spouse as the beneficiary of the account, it can be directed to an IRA Trust for the spouse's benefit. The trust can then mandatorily distribute required distributions each year (or more often, or leave it in the discretion of the Trustee) to the spouse. The Trustee can also be given discretion to provide more money if the spouse requests it. But what benefits are there to handling it through the IRA Trust?

- If your spouse dies before you, the contingent beneficiaries of the trust can "redirect" the IRA funds to the other beneficiaries you have chosen;

- If your spouse dies after you but before all of the funds are used, then the remainder of the IRA Trust goes to your other chosen beneficiaries; and

- The trust funds are protected from your spouse's creditors, bankruptcy, lawsuits, and other outside legal forces.

If the retirement account goes directly to your spouse, then they can spend it all, choose different beneficiaries than you should they pass on before the money is gone, and while there are some legal protections for spousal IRAs during their lifetime the creditors can come after the remainder when they pass on. With the Spousal IRA Trust, these unwanted contingencies are eliminated.

Chapter Eleven:
The Complete Divorce Firewall Strategy

Aimee had no idea what she was doing in a lawyer's office at 25 years old, but she trusted Uncle Rick and Uncle Rob. Well. Rick was her uncle on her mother's side, and Rob was their cousin. However, Aimee grew up always calling them both "uncle." She trusted them both, and when she graduated with her M.B.A. and landed her first real job, a present from her uncles was them paying for a strategy session with their attorney. The four of them sat around a large conference room table, and it was Uncle Rob who began.

"Aimee, I know you have probably heard some of what happened when I divorced Stacy," he said matter of factly. "I'm sure you haven't heard all of it, though."

"All I know is what I heard from my mom, and she said it was messy," Aimee replied.

The three men laughed out loud.

"What's so funny?" Aimee asked.

"Aimee, I'm your uncles' attorney Chuck Ocean, and I can assure you that the divorce was most certainly not messy," the attorney said.

"But Aunt Stacy had called mom several times, and it always ended up with her screaming into the phone," Aimee said.

"Chuck didn't say that Stacy liked the terms of the divorce," Rick said. *"He just said it wasn't messy."*

"That's why we wanted to bring you here," Rob said. *"From the start, I made sure that I was protecting myself from all of the ridiculousness in the world so I could grow and build my future without anyone trying to take it away from me. That's why when I was about your age I came to Mr. Ocean here, and he helped me set up a trust and begin a system to ward off lawsuits, creditors, and all other kinds of legal and financial disasters, including a potential future divorce. It was all planned out ahead of time."*

"By creating the strategy, maintaining it over time, and adding to it, I was able to keep everything I worked for and saved from Stacy during the divorce," Rob continued. *"That's why there was no hesitation in filing for divorce when Stacy cheated on me."*

"She cheated on you!" Aimee practically yelled. *"I had no idea."*

"Well, neither did your mom the first few times Stacy called, but I set her straight," Rick said. *"After that, your mom blocked Stacy's number."*

"The point is that I kept everything I worked for and built because I had this 'firewall strategy' in place long before it was needed," Rob continued. *"In the divorce, Stacy kept her stuff, but the only thing she saved of her own money during fifteen years of marriage is the house she's now living in and her 401k. I kept all of the rental properties, the investments, everything. The right combination of a Domestic Asset Protection Trust, corporate entities, and a solid prenuptial agreement that kept these assets separate made all of the difference in the world."*

"And that's why you're here," Chuck said. *"Your uncles want to make sure you get your own trust put in place now and build on that as life progresses. When the time comes, we'll look at cohabitation agreements, prenups, and other protections to secure your wealth for you, and eventually your children."*

"Whoa, children?" Aimee said, looking a little overwhelmed. "My boyfriend and I have only just started talking about moving in together. We're a long way off from marriage let alone children."

"You mean your boyfriend, the artist, who is still looking for work?" Rick said more than asked.

"Sounds like it isn't too soon to also talk about that cohabitation agreement," Chuck said.

This is the chapter you have probably been waiting for. We've gone through the problems of marriage and divorce, the different planning elements available, and more in-depth analysis of the legal documents and strategies. Here is where we tie it all together at the end using our hero Rob Paulson's situation as an example of how to do things the right way.

As a refresher, Rob Paulson married Stacy and had three children before getting divorced when his wife cheated with a coworker. Fortunately for Rob, he kept all of his assets, got joint and equal custody of his children, and only had to pay Stacy the appropriate child support required under state law. So how exactly did he accomplish this? Since this is a hypothetical, we can examine an overall plan with three different levels of effectiveness before showing how Rob maximized the Divorce Firewall Strategy for him and his children.

The first level is the Basic Divorce Firewall Strategy to provide what should be considered the new baseline protection incorporating only the required elements. The second level is the Advanced Divorce Firewall Strategy and provides more comprehensive protection planning using corporate entities and advanced estate planning documents. Finally, the third level is the Generational Divorce Firewall Strategy that not only provides protection to you for your lifetime, but it also extends that protection another generation so your wealth is protected for your children from their potential divorces, bankruptcies, lawsuits, and even loss of any disability benefits so any remaining wealth makes it to your grandchildren.

Level 1 Basic

Rob Paulson started out having elements of both the basic and advanced plans when he got involved with Stacy and long before the three children came along. If we put aside the corporate protection he had for his financial firm, Rob still did more than enough to cover himself compared to most people who rely solely on a one-time, attorney-generated premarital agreement. Rob certainly did a lot better than downloading a pre-marital agreement, or doing nothing at all like Bill Peterson did. Here's the outline of the basic plan and how it works:

Before Engagement

- Cohabitation Agreement executed so all finances are kept separate, expenses and chores for the common household are shared as agreed, and it is clearly stated that this living arrangement is not to be a substitute or precursor to marriage;

- The terms of the agreement are followed, and the partner also follows the terms;

- The Cohabitation Agreement and its terms were reviewed periodically, at least annually and certainly is any major situations change; and

- A Domestic Asset Protection Trust is enacted, and any investment wealth is placed in the trust with each paycheck.

This should also be the stage when at least the basic estate planning documents are put in place. A financial power of attorney and health care power of attorney are both created to name agents to act on your behalf in the event of incapacity, and a Will and Revocable Living Trust to direct all of your assets to your chosen beneficiaries in the event of death. Of course, the terms of the Domestic Asset Protection Trust will also name beneficiaries for the assets owned by that trust.

Before becoming engaged, it is also critical to make sure that your partner knows and understands that any marriage WILL have a comprehensive Pre-Marital Agreement in place along with keeping their assets separate, that you will not consider marriage without one, and if that is a problem you can just continue or part ways. Ensuring that you have the discussion early enough in the relationship means it won't be some big surprise if marriage is discussed and a prenup becomes a big topic of conversation.

Engagement But Before Marriage

All of the steps previously taken as well as the elements put in place before the engagement are continued, but now is the time to take steps to ensure that marriage will only take place if the Divorce Firewall Strategy is followed. The following additional steps should now be taken:

- Both of you discuss a Pre-Marital Agreement with your attorneys, all of the terms are agreed upon; and the document is executed well in advance of the marriage;

- Part of the prenup process should be disclosure of the existence of the Domestic Asset Protection Trust, but disclosure of the assets in the trust are subject to negotiations and it needs to be clear that the assets of the trust are never to be considered marital property; and

---

- Terms regarding future children should not be ignored just because you don't have children yet or that you both may not currently want children (in fact, the fact that you may both want to forgo children should be in the agreement, but nonetheless address the subject of children in the prenup.)

After Marriage

The wedding has come and gone, and now life continues with your spouse. This doesn't mean that the planning is done. In fact, these steps are just as critical as having the Basic Divorce Firewall Strategy enacted in the first place. In fact, a court could throw out the whole plan if you simply let the terms slip away and start combining your assets and living life like Bill Peterson did. Here's what needs to happen to reinforce the strategy:

- Maintain regular transfers of your excess paychecks into the Domestic Asset Protection Trust. DO NOT be talked into using your wealth to pay for vacations, home improvements and furniture, and expenses for the children that are out of line with the premarital agreement. If extras for the children are to be split evenly between you, then enforce that. If paying for household furnishings and home upgrades are to be split in proportion to your pay, then insist on that. If the costs of vacations are to be alternately paid for by each of you, then stick to that. It becomes a fatal failing to simply pay for things yourself because your spouse starts telling you "You make more money so you can afford it:"

- Revisit the Premarital Agreement on a regular basis, and at a minimum every five years, or right away if there is a major changed circumstance such as someone's income greatly increasing or decreasing. In all cases, both of you should continue to use different attorneys to negotiate any changes in the agreement, and execute them on time; and

- NEVER, NEVER, NEVER AGREE TO LET YOUR SPOUSE STOP WORKING. Too many times, a marriage starts to slip into complacency, and a spouse starts to think they can relax. In the case of wives, as they get older their friends end up stopping work after a child is born, and they start to think that if their friends can do it, then they should be entitled to stop working as well regardless of what the prenup said. In the case of men with busy but highly successful women, the men may start to pick up some slack with home chores and begin to believe they're entitled to quit their job because their wife is making "so much more money" than they are. If your spouse quits or loses their job and intentionally drags their feet in finding another job for more than a few months, then it is time to walk away. NEVER let your spouse become so dependent on you that if the marriage breaks up a court has to decide whether the government pays for their support, or you will… because you will lose in that decision every time.

With these steps in the Basic Divorce Firewall Strategy, you will be doing better than 99.9% of people getting married who are later divorced. The major point here is that the work doesn't end with the documents being in place. You need to have the discipline to continue to do everything the strategy calls for.

Level 2 Advanced

Bringing the Divorce Firewall Strategy to another level includes all of the Basic steps while adding some that should be considered a part of general financial growth and asset protection for the more confident and ambitious among us. However, these steps need to be taken in coordination with your Domestic Asset Protection Trust and cognizant of the terms of the Pre-Marital Agreement.

- Incorporate businesses you are involved in, whether it is a corporation, limited liability company, or other entity, and have the shares/interests be owned by the Domestic Asset Protection Trust;

- If there are children, then having your own revocable living trust be the beneficiary of the policy can protect your children through the age of majority in line with any obligations listed in the pre-marital agreement while making sure that any excess insurance proceeds go to the beneficiaries you want rather than just paying to your spouse. This also means your named trustee is handling the money to make sure it is being used the right way;

- Find a sensible way for your major personal assets to be classified as business assets and place them into a corporate entity to also be owned by the Domestic Asset Protection Trust. This may also provide you some lawsuit and liability protection by leasing assets like your vehicles back to you through that corporate entity; and

- If you and your spouse are living in a property owned by your Domestic Asset Protection Trust and your premarital agreement states that rent and expenses are to be divided, then have the residence owned inside a corporate entity inside the trust and then execute a lease for you and your spouse. Now you and your spouse are diverting some money into your Domestic Asset Protection Trust through that corporate entity.

These suggestions are usually independently considered good ideas for asset protection, but in the case of corporate entities there now is a second layer of protection between your assets and people you don't want to get them.

Level 3 Generational

If you have successfully enacted all of the elements of the Basic and Advanced strategy, and you are happy with the results, then it is time to consider passing the same type of protection to the next generation. Here are the added strategy pieces:

- For estate planning, instead of leaving your estate directly to your children, enact Asset Management Trusts for each child so that your Domestic Asset Protection Trust and Revocable Living Trust can direct all of your non-retirement wealth into a protected trust for your child's lifetime. Now the trust can protect your wealth from any threats to your children like divorce, lawsuits, bankruptcy, creditors, and disability. If your child wants to buy a house, then their trustee can purchase the house in the name of the Asset Management Trust and allow them to live there.

In addition, the trustee can take a cue from the Advanced section and place the house in a corporate structure and rent the house to your child and their spouse to increase the eventual inheritance to your grandchildren;

- To both protect your child and maximize inherited income tax savings, instead of naming your children or their Asset Management Trust as beneficiary of your retirement accounts, create IRA Trusts for each of your children and name those IRA Trusts as beneficiary. Now the trustee is able to stretch the income taxes over the maximum time allowed by law (usually ten years) resulting in lower overall income taxes yet still protect the money from divorce, lawsuits, bankruptcy, creditors, and disability. (These trusts can also be structured to turn over all of the trust assets to the child's corresponding Asset Management Trust when all of the potential tax benefits have been achieved.)

Now that we have covered the three levels of the Divorce Firewall Strategy, let's take a look at how the Generational plan played out over Rob Paulson's life.

- Rob Paulson started out knowing how to protect himself and his assets for himself. He had heard too many stories of people losing most of their life's work in a divorce where people didn't plan ahead. His father made sure he understood that there was never going to be a relationship guarantee, and he had to make sure that he hedged his bets. That is why as soon as he was out of graduate school and able to put away money, he set up his own Wyoming Domestic Asset Protection Trust and set up his investments inside the trust. With the help of his cousin/best friend Rick acting as Trustee, Rob started putting away after-tax dollars in mutual funds, an annuity, a bank account, and some short-term CDs. In addition, by the time Rob was ready to go out on his own and establish his financial planning firm, he did so by having Rick set up a Wyoming Limited Liability Company, and the starter funds from the trust got Rob started.

- When Rob eventually met Stacy, he spent a long time getting to know her and not becoming exclusive for more than a year. When they were ready to do so, Rob sat Stacy down to explain exactly what he expected out of a committed relationship, and he was firm that the deeper the relationship got, the firmer the contractual paperwork would get. He explained how his father lost out in his divorce, and, while he cares a lot for Stacy, he knew that feelings change, and he was not going to risk everything he built. Stacy was a little put off by such a frank conversation, but she understood. There were no illusions about some "happily ever after" happening without a prenup and finances being separate, but since she always intended to keep working on her career even in the event of marriage and kids, it didn't matter to her.

- Once Rob and Stacy had been exclusive for a year, Stacy started hinting at moving in together. Rob was still fairly busy taking his business to the next level, but he saw a lot of benefits in living together... provided the paperwork was handled. That's when Rob reminded her of the "paperwork discussion," that they would need a cohabitation agreement for living in a house he would buy, and that he had to "talk to his Trustee first." At this point, Rob had accumulated enough in his Domestic Asset Protection Trust to purchase a small house, so Rick formed another LLC in the name of the trust, transferred the money into the LLC, and Rob and Stacy went house hunting with Rick. When they found the right house at the right price and after both Rob and Stacy spoke with their respective attorneys, Rob and Stacy executed the cohabitation agreement and lease at the same time Rick was signing the paperwork buying the house into the LLC. Part of the cohabitation agreement was that Stacy would be paying her half of the rent to the LLC, and Rob would likewise be paying his half of the rent. It was also at this time that both Rob and Rick encouraged Stacy to look at buying her own house to rent out so she could start building her own real estate portfolio.

- After a few years of living together, Stacy started hinting at marriage. Rob was prepared for this discussion to come up, and he and Stacy had both started to accumulate their own separate assets. Before approaching Stacy about her "hints," Rob spoke with his attorney to start on a premarital agreement. When Rob finally discussed marriage with Stacy, it was not a straight-out proposal with some elaborate romantic gesture of getting down on one knee with a beach sunset in the background. It was at their kitchen table with all of the same starkness of their discussions about first becoming exclusive and then executing the cohabitation agreement. He mentioned the premarital agreement and all of the things they would have to work out before he would even propose. After several months of back and forth with their respective attorneys, they had an agreeable premarital agreement in place... and then a few weeks later Rob gave Stacy the romantic proposal on the beach.

- Five years have passed since Rob and Stacy were married, and they now have two children. Stacy had talked about giving up her job and staying home with the children, but Rob reminded them of their Premarital Agreement as well as the recent update, and she agreed that she was going to continue to work and financially contribute to the household. There were a ton of excuses and complaints, mainly about how none of her friends had to work and their husbands didn't make nearly as much as he did, how the kids would benefit from her being at home, and how she could cater to his needs more if he would just let her stay home. Finally, Rob told her "We agreed that we would both financially contribute to the family, so if you are going to break your word on that, then I might as well divorce you and find someone else to be with who will keep her word." That was the end of that discussion.

- Ten years after that, meaning fifteen years and three kids after Rob married Stacy, Rob started to get a strange feeling about Stacy. She was just acting different. He talked to his father about it, and when Rob had finished describing the situation, his father just sighed. "This is exactly how it was with your mother," he said. "Get a private investigator now."

Rob hired one of the best local PIs available, and he gathered more than enough evidence that Stacy was cheating on him with one of her coworkers and presented it to Rob. Rob kept his cool, and the first people he called were his lawyer and his Trustee, Rick. This was going to be at least a 30-day process, so Rob got started as soon as he could. He called into his office to have his meetings rescheduled, and he began packing. By 3 p.m., Rob's dad had picked up the kids to take them to his place, the movers had packed all of Rob's stuff to move into storage, and Rick had a process server provide Stacy with the standard 30-day eviction notice. Rob temporarily moved into the vacation house in the name of his Domestic Asset Protection Trust, and the only evidence that he ever lived at the house was the folder of pictures of Stacy and her lover that the PI took resting right in the middle of the kitchen table. He ignored all of Stacy's calls that night, and the next day, until Stacy's own attorney called to let her know that Rob's attorney contacted them to start the divorce process.

Within 30 days, Rob was back in the house his trust's LLC owned with a brand-new lease just in his name, the kids' bedrooms remained largely untouched, and all of Stacy's belongings had been moved to her own house.

Here's what happened with the terms of the divorce:

- Rob's house was never on the chopping block because it was purchased by his trust through an LLC, Stacy was never on the deed, so Rob didn't own the house for it to be considered in a divorce even if the premarital agreement hadn't also excluded it;

- Rob kept the vacation house purchased with inherited money, because he put the money into his trust, and his trustee purchased the vacation home through a newly created LLC;

- Rob kept all of his investments since the excess money from his paycheck and distributions from his firm also went into the trust to purchase those investments (and Stacy kept her more limited but still significant separate investments);

- Rob kept all of his vehicles because all of them were owned through corporate entities in the trust;

- Rob kept his retirement and Stacy kept hers, because that's what was in the premarital agreement;

- Rob pays no alimony because that was also in the premarital agreement, and because Stacy never stopped working despite some inclinations and prodding of Rob to do so;

- Rob is paying some child support because he earns much more than his now ex-wife does, but he always knew that would happen;

- Rob and Stacy have equal joint custody because that is also what they agreed to in the premarital agreement, the judge found no reason to alter that;

- Stacy's coworker was actually a senior member of her team, meaning he was fraternizing with a subordinate, so he was fired, and Stacy was reassigned to a less desirable position but at the same pay and hours;

- The kids are old enough that they understand what happened without Rob even having to tell them, and they resent their mother for breaking up the family; and

- While Rob and Stacy are technically equally sharing custody, the children, particularly the oldest, chooses to spend more time with Rob.

It would be nothing more than a revenge fantasy to say that Stacy was miserable and broke for the rest of her life, but the fact that she followed the encouraged to keep building up her own assets, so she was much more financially stable on her own than many divorcees. She had a few rental properties of her own that did well enough to more than pay the mortgage and cover the rent she was paying in a more modest apartment until the lease on one of the houses was up, and she moved into that soon after. While a divorce should never be considered a "success story," in this case Rob and Stacy both came out OK, but Rob came out a lot better than most higher earners in a divorce do.

As you can see, the Basic Divorce Firewall Strategy in itself is a remarkable upgrade from simply executing a premarital agreement before marriage and keeping your fingers crossed. But that's not all it can do to protect you once you factor in other asset protection and liability protection steps in an Advanced strategy, not to mention protection for your loved ones after you are gone through a Generational strategy. Whichever level of protection you choose to work with, it certainly has to be better than flipping a coin to see if you become part of the 50% divorce statistics and have your hard-earned fortune left to the mercy of an uncaring court.